To Dianne,
Wishing you
happiness,
Gilda Q. Young

Excerpts from Others Who Have Shared Their Insights to Lasting Happiness

"To me, happiness is a profoundly affirmative experience of self and of life. I do not think of anything "making" me happy. I find my two greatest sources of joy in my work and in my marriage. I am passionately committed to both. I sustain happiness in these two spheres while striving to operate at a high level of awareness. I say "strive" because I do not always succeed. I am consciously committed to being happy and that takes a kind of discipline. In my experience, when faced with suffering, it is often useful to ask: 'Is this trip necessary?' Pretty soon, my love of life and my normal high spirits are back at the forefront of my consciousness."

–Nathaniel Branden,
Psychologist and Author of many books on self-esteem

"I have a boat and a farm with horses—two lifelong dreams—and the knowledge that I can get anything I want. What makes me happiest is when I can help with the misfortune of family and friends."

–Morgan Freeman, Actor

"When I'm happy I really don't have to think about it. It's when I'm unhappy that I think about it. So when I'm happy, time goes by and the question of why I'm happy never comes up."

–Paul Orfalea, Founder/Chairperson of Kinko's

"Life makes me happy, every sign of it...a bud, a leaf, a child, anything that reflects the mystery and the beauty of life itself."

–Diane Von Furstenberg, Businesswoman

"I have a great family, a wife to whom I've been married for 35 years, two children, a wonderful daughter-in-law, a wonderful son-in-law, a grandson, two great pups (Shih-tzus); everyone's healthy; and a career that pretty much went according to early, ambitious plans. HOWEVER, I'm neurotic as the next guy and I well know what free-floating anxiety is. So, if I am happier than most people, it is because I remind myself constantly that I have no reason to be otherwise. And, further, because in my wife's words: I have always been the king of denial."

–Hal Prince, Director

"There are moments of happiness that come from something external —finishing a piece of writing, seeing someone's life change for the better, dancing—but those that are most complete seem to be the moments of feeling skinless, a part of the universe, and those moments of happiness can come unexpectedly while doing errands or just walking on a sunny day."

–Gloria Steinem, Author and Feminist Activist

"Enjoying time with my friends and family, and being successful doing work that I love makes me happy."

–Alan Menken, Composer

"Happiness is a choice; each moment I can choose to be happy regardless of my circumstances, or I can give my situation power to dictate my happiness quotient."

--Cherie Carter-Scott, Ph.D.,
Consultant, Speaker, Author of *If Life Is a Game, These Are the Rules*

Happiness
Instruction Kit

No Assembly Required

Willa A. Young
Marriage & Family Therapist

Foreword by **Jack Canfield**,
Co-author of *Chicken Soup for the Soul*® series

Published by:
The Williams Group
P.O. Box 3692
Santa Barbara, California 93103

Copyright © 2002 by Willa A. Young

All rights reserved. No part of this book may be reproduced or transmitted in
any form or by any means electronic or mechanical, including photocopying,
recording or by any information storage and retrieval system, without written
permission from the publisher.

ISBN: 0-9710683-8-0

Publisher's Cataloging-in-Publication
(Provided by Quality Books, Inc.)

Young, Willa A.
     Happiness instruction kit: no assembly required /
Willa A. Young — 1st ed.
     p. cm.
     Includes bibliographical references.

     1. Happiness. 2. Conduct of life.   1. Title.

BJ1481.Y68 2001   158
                   QBI01-700422

Editor: Gail M. Kearns, GMK Editorial & Writing Services, Santa Barbara, CA
Copyeditor: Barbara Coster, Cross-t.i Copyediting, Santa Barbara, CA
Cover & Interior Design: Peri Poloni, Knockout Design, Cameron Park, CA
www.knockoutbooks.com

To my mother,

Meryl Ruben A. Young,

who taught me

the true meaning

of happiness

Contents
Happiness Kit Tools

Foreword

No matter how many books we have read, tapes we have listened to or seminars we have attended, we all need to be reminded of what to do to maintain happiness, joy, and bliss in life. These states are not only available to the mystics and those who live in California, but to all of us—each and every one. Many pioneers in psychology and the human potential movement have discovered the techniques—many simple, many profound—that can be used by all of us to create lasting happiness, true joy, and deep inner peace. Willa has done us all the favor of gathering these techniques into one source that we can all refer to on a daily basis to re-mind (literally to give ourselves a new mind) ourselves of what is possible if we will just attend to it and focus on it.

Every person deserves to have more joy in life. We were born to experience pleasure and joy. It is our birthright. But somewhere along the way most of us lost our way. We became so preoccupied with the day-to-day rat race of our lives that we forgot how to inject our lives with the experience of happiness. Willa's *Happiness Instruction Kit: No Assembly Required* reminds us to take each moment—and with very little extra effort—fill it with joy.

The power of this book is that the things she suggests that we do are both simple and powerful. The instructions are straight-forward and easy to understand. Willa reminds us that we already have everything we need inside of ourselves to create all of the happiness we truly want.

You have begun an important journey by picking up this book and reading this far. Make sure you give yourself the gift of fin-ishing this book and putting the principles and techniques into action. A wise man once said, "You can't hire other people to do your push-ups for you." Likewise, you cannot hire someone else to put the ideas in this book into action for you. The results are up to you. If you are willing to read, assimilate and get into action, you can be as happy as you want to be. What are you waiting for? Turn the page now and create a life full of happiness!

Jack Canfield,
Co-author of *Chicken Soup for the Soul®* series

Acknowledgments

I would like to thank the numerous people who supported me in this project and believed I had this book inside me all along.

Bill Shapiro, my wonderful husband, whose love, support, and encouragement allowed me to write this book.

Beaumont Shapiro, my son, who gave his time, energy, ideas, and most of all his love. There is no greater happiness than you.

Gail Kearns, my editor. She receives my special gratitude, appreciation and thanks for all of her help and devotion in bringing this book to completion.

Jack Canfield, to whom I am grateful for writing the Foreword.

Patty Aubery, for her guidance. Thank you!

To Dad, my love and gratitude.

Linda Serbin and Jeril Lewis, my sisters, who continuously gave me their input and ideas.

Howard Greenfield, my uncle, whose sense of humor and guidance provided me with endless ideas of happiness. He showed me what happiness looked like.

William Ruben, my late uncle Billy, who was always proud of me and loved me unconditionally.

Nelsa Gidney, my friend since grade school, who read through countless versions of the manuscript, giving them her editorial touch.

Judy Pearl, my college roommate, who gave the manuscript her love and time.

Thanks also to those whose contributions ensured the completion of this book: Shandra Belknap, Hal Zina Bennett, Art Bentley, Nathaniel Branden, Richard Carlson, Cherie Carter-Scott, Carol Clement, Barbara Coster, Terri Duncan, Morgan Freeman, Diane Von Furstenberg, Betty Hatch, Nancy Kanter, Roberta Kimmel, Bobbi Kroot, Lori Leahy, Karen Levy, Alan Menken, Ryan Miner, Martha Mullins, Ruth Nebel, Megan Patton, Hal Prince, Marty Rubinstein, Ruth Silverman, Gloria Steinem, Julie Stephen, and Bruce Williams.

And to my students and clients throughout the years who have allowed me into their lives and provided me with inspiration.

Introduction

I was born into a house of mourning. Four months before I was born, my father was killed in World War II. Just a little more than a week after my birth, a stranger in a uniform came to our door again, carrying a yellow telegram. This time it was for my grandmother, who lived with us. Her eighteen-year-old son was missing in action, presumed dead.

The war had taken my father and my uncle, and the smell of death hung in the air. The sadness and grief were palpable. Yet, in the midst of it there was reason to celebrate. A young life had come into the house: me. And besides, there was my three-year-old sister Linda, who brought a certain liveliness to the adults whose lives had been so badly mangled by the war.

At this point you may be thinking that this is a strange way to start a book about bringing happiness into your life. I gave that a lot of thought before I started, and what I realized was that even in the midst of much grief and sadness, the human spirit seems to seek happiness. This is difficult to remember when life feels indeed dark and even hopeless. But perhaps the first step toward happiness is the realization that bringing joy into our lives does not depend wholly on external events.

I had no memory of my father, but my mother talked about him a lot when we were growing up. She said that she wanted us to know the kind of man he was. I know now that she idealized him, that no human being could possibly be as good as he was. Though my father might have been gone in the flesh, I still had a fantasy father who loved me and, at least in my mind, was far more perfect than any of my friends' fathers. Though fantasy fathers can't put their arms around you when you need encouragement or love, these early fantasies did teach me the power of our minds to change our experience of our lives.

I guided my behavior according to what I believed my father would think. Would he approve? What would he think of where I went to college, or whom I chose to marry? I wanted to honor him and carry on his legacy, one he would be proud of.

Being born right after the death of my father, I felt a huge responsibility. Was I to act as a replacement? My father's name was William Ira Adelman; my name was Willa Ina Adelman. Every birthday I felt guilt and sadness about me being alive and my father being dead for the same number of years.

I would have given anything to see my biological father for just five minutes. Did I look like him? How did his voice sound? Did he smell like a dad? All my life I longed to feel his strong arms around me. This desire has given me an understanding of the inner drives of adopted children who search for their birth parents, and for parents and children who have been estranged from one another for years. There is a sense of deep curiosity and yearning to feel a bond.

My father painted beautiful oil paintings. I remember when I was about nine years old, alone in my room painting. I could not get the paint to do what I wanted. The colors were not mixing right. I thought, "If only my father were here, he would know how to teach me and then I could fix it. He would be here with me, guiding my hand over the canvas."

When I was older, I was told that my sister Linda would ask my mother, "How come everyone else's daddy came back from the war and mine didn't?" My mother's heart was already broken. No pain is worse than feeling that of your own child's.

My mother remarried when I was two years old, which meant at last my sister Linda and I had a father.

Often when a child loses a parent, she fears that something will happen to the surviving parent, leaving the child alone. This can be terrifying. The fear stays with you. This certainly was true for me. The thought would run through my mind, "What would happen to me if my mother died?" The way I dealt with this fear was to be the best little girl I could be. In this way, I thought mother would be happy. I would never bring her pain. She had lost enough. And, somehow, in my mind, the happiness I brought her would guarantee that she would never die.

I never wanted to feel the pain of loss, the kind my mother endured. I devised a plan to prevent this from ever happening to me. I vowed to myself never to fall in love. However, what I did not realize was that by putting this wall of isolation around myself, to protect myself from loss, there was no way love and happiness could enter my life. Isolation brings loneliness. You pretend you're okay, but inside you know the truth.

I was extremely shy as a child. I have vivid memories of hanging on to my mother's leg. I didn't want her to leave me. I was not about to go to kindergarten without her, not me. I never talked to any of the children in first grade, not a one. I only spoke to the teacher.

There were other contributing factors to unhappiness in my childhood. I was diagnosed with Perthes disease, an illness that affects the bones. I spent six weeks in a leg cast from my waist to my toe. When the heavy cast was removed, by cutting through the whitish, by now dirty plaster, I saw my leg and I fainted. My leg had shrunk; it wa

had one normal leg and one spind

Here I was, a lonely shy girl, feel

me—"Poor Willa, born after her

friends, afraid of life, never wantii

and now I had a spindle for a leg. \
_____ .... your

own two feet, it's easy to feel overwhelmed. I was.

I had intense physical therapy and wore a cold metal leg brace. It
made a loud squeaking sound every time I took a step. This was
the type of brace worn by kids who had had polio. I felt different
from the other children. I didn't fit in. I was gawky looking, lonely, didn't have polio but was treated as if I did. I wanted desperately for the kids to like and accept me, but they didn't. I had no
self-confidence and zero social skills. I was not happy.

I grew up. Time passes and the world doesn't seem to care if we
are happy or not. My mother taught me social skills so I learned
to interact with others. As alienated as I felt from the world, I did
well academically. I graduated from Stephens College and
Columbia University. I was sure my dad would have been proud.

In my early twenties, I married. I thought if I got married, I
would be happy. Aren't all brides happy? I remember sitting on
the floor and crying as a young bride, filled with disappointment
and thinking, "Is this all there is?" Still in my twenties, I divorced.

al pain seeped steadily through the wall I had put myself. One day, while shopping at the supermarket, I y shopping cart and ran to the public telephone, where I antically began searching the yellow pages for a therapist. I knew I needed help. I remember thinking, "Surely everyone doesn't live in silent pain the way I do. There must be happy people in the world." Looking back, I now recognize how desperate I had been in that moment, consulting the yellow pages for someone to help me.

This was a critical time for me. I just knew there had to be another way to live, be joyous and carefree and happy in the world. However, I did not know how to get to that point. I made the decision to spend time in therapy getting to know myself.

After time and much self-study, my life started to change. I slowly began to gain confidence and soon was convinced that happiness was possible. It was at this time that I cut the attachment with my father. He was dead. I was alive and it was my time for me to live. That defining moment changed the way I looked at my life. My life continues to be an adventure. I am now happily married, with a wonderful husband and wonderful teenage son.

I tell you my story not to gain your sympathy, but because I want you to know that I understand how it feels to be unhappy, sad, and lonely. I was certainly not born into happiness. It was not external events but my own ongoing search of myself that enabled me to become a happy person. But I am also just as human as you are. There are days when happiness eludes me, too. I continue to learn about myself, to seek ways to be happier.

I never thought about writing a book about all this. The idea never crossed my mind. Why would I want to undertake such a thing? The reason to write came in 1996 after my mother died. She was my teacher, mentor, and friend. Suddenly, I felt compelled to write this book. I had to tell the world the lessons my mother taught me.

I immediately realized that if Mother could die, then I would also die. Would I have any regrets if I died tomorrow? YES, the answer came to me. The only regret I would have is that I never wrote a book to tell people what I had learned from my mother. Telling others what I knew about happiness could perhaps help them find the happiness we all deserve.

With the tools I pass along to you in these pages, you too can find happiness. It is with this conviction that I have written this book—to assure you that whatever situation you are in at this moment, you have the power to improve it, to create opportunities to experience the happiness you seek.

Start Now—
Wherever You Are—
on Your Happiness
Adventure

Happiness is not a state to arrive at, but a manner of traveling.
—Margaret Lee Runbeck

Picture this scenario: You're going on your dream vacation. You've arranged for vacation time. You cancel the newspaper and ask a neighbor to collect your mail while you're away. Then you get your suitcase out, pack some clothes, grab your passport—don't forget your Happiness Instruction Kit!—and take a cab to the airport.

At the airport, you start getting excited as you near the ticket counter. After all, this *is* your dream vacation! You step up to the counter. The ticket agent greets you with a smile and asks for your ticket. You don't have a ticket. The agent is patient and asks you what your destination is, but you hadn't thought about that. You smile at the agent and tell her you're not sure. She gives you a puzzled look.

By now, you notice a long line of other passengers forming behind you who need to check in for their flights. The agent remains patient and suggests that you might want to take a trip to a place where you can relax on the beach. You're still not sure, so she suggests Paris, where there are plenty of sights to marvel at and many things to do. You think for a second, but dismiss the idea. You don't have a clue where you want to go! Well then, for sure you can't get there.

What you desperately need to do now is to decide where you want to go. You take out your Happiness Instruction Kit, which gives you directions to the way to happiness. You tell the ticket agent you want a ticket to happiness—the place where you can forget all your troubles and feel better about yourself. She replies that they don't fly there, it's a different kind of journey. You reach into your kit again and take out your compass. You smile at the ticket agent, thank her for her time, and head in the direction of happiness. You've taken the first step on a new journey.

I look at my entire life as a journey. There are times when I feel I'm on an adventure and need a machete to blaze a new trail. At other times, I'm on a cruise, smoothly sailing the open seas and charting my next course in life. It's the expedition of life, or the process of living, that brings happiness. Everyone's life is a journey. Each of us travels our own personal path looking for some meaning in life. This can be different for all of us, but generally it has to do with participating in life and knowing that because we're here, we make a difference.

The highway to happiness is not hard to find. The road to happiness is in front of you if only you would look in the right direction. Imagine walking or riding along a road, enjoying the scenery. You're not thinking about your arrival; you're totally absorbed in what you're doing. Your mind is in the present. It's not thinking about what you did yesterday, or about all you have to do tomorrow. You're here NOW, and each present moment leads to the next one. You're in the flow of life.

The journey to happiness is an ongoing, captivating trip. You don't reach happiness and then stop with the expectation of staying there forever. Invariably, you have to strive to make happiness a priority in your life. You must remain conscious and ask yourself, "Will this decision make me happy?" Remember, it's not the destination of happiness that we need to think about, but rather the process of living and what we do while we're traveling in our daily lives.

Happiness is experienced along the way of your journey. To illustrate, think of marathon runners who run 26.2 miles. This is quite a race. It requires extensive mental and physical training, yet the runners cross the finish line in a second and the event is over. But what about all the miles they ran for several hours prior to crossing the finish line? It's having run those miles that brought them to the finish line.

A few years ago in Los Angeles, when I ran with the Santa Monica Track Club, I researched marathon runners. I interviewed several of the top long-distance runners, who averaged a mile in five to six-and-a-half minutes. I was curious about what they did with their minds while they ran. Before the survey, I had thought that these top runners would be playing Beethoven in their heads or counting posts along the way—anything to take their minds off what they were doing.

I found just the opposite. The top runners who ran at Olympic pace had their minds focused in the present moment during the entire event. They were totally aware of their bodies and how far they had run. The opposite was true of the slower runners. They didn't concentrate on the marathon. They played music in their heads, sang songs, did anything to get their minds off what they were doing. From this I concluded that when we're focused on what we're doing, we enjoy the experience, are more efficient and excel at what we do.

Many people would be happier if they didn't think so much about happiness. "Am I happy yet? Yes, but am I REALLY happy?" These are questions my clients ask themselves. But there's a danger in overanalyzing anything, especially happiness. So give your mind a holiday and just experience the NOW. If every moment of your life isn't filled with BLISS, accept it. All journeys have detours; getting back on track is part of your job in life.

Start to think of your life as an adventure. It's the exploration of your journey that will bring you happiness. Think of all the people you'll meet along the way and the places you'll travel to. You don't even have to leave home to experience happiness and a sense of well-being.

When you find what you love doing and then create a life where you can do it more than fifty percent of the time, happiness will follow. Your life will take on new meaning. Remember, you have a lifetime warranty for happiness. So why not become the happiest person you know!

Define Happiness for YOURSELF!

But what is happiness except the simple harmony between a man and the life he leads.

–Albert Camus

Happiness for sale! A television commercial promotes a shiny new BMW zipping around mountain curves. Suddenly, the words "Happiness is not around the corner. Happiness *is* the corner" appear on the screen. Are car makers taking a Zen approach to selling cars? "Be Happy, Drive Happy" is a recent ad for the Alamo car rental company. "Visit Disneyland, the happiest place on earth," promotes another ad with happiness as its theme. Have you taken a walk down the center aisle of your local department store lately—the section where they sell all the beauty and makeup products? If so, you might have caught sight of Clinique's ad campaign, "C'mon, Get Happy!" What gives? Why is everyone hyping happiness? Who's happy? What counts as happiness anyway?

Who's really happiest? According to one poll, published in *USA Weekend*, "two-thirds of Americans say they are very happy. On a scale of 1 to 10, one-fifth give themselves a perfect 10. The average rating is a high 7.8 regardless of race or sex." Regarding happiness, the poll reports, "Americans' priorities are clear: Good health, strong faith and love are more important than material wealth or fame." Only four percent say a high income is the most important ingredient in determining their happiness. Religious faith and spirituality (forty-seven percent) is the one most significant element in personal happiness after health. Thirty-eight percent say being loved makes them the happiest. If you're saying to yourself, "But I don't know what makes me happy; I'm not even sure I'd know happiness if it fell on me," now is the time to think about it and define it for yourself. First, you must picture yourself as if you were happy. Then ask yourself:

What do I feel like?

What do I act like?

What is my attitude like?

Perhaps you'd be less critical of yourself. Or maybe you'd offer to help other people more than you're doing now. You might recognize the humor in life and not take yourself so seriously.

What exactly do you think you need to achieve happiness? Many people report they're happy when they feel their life has meaning and purpose. Keep in mind, though, that everyone has a different idea about what makes them happy.

My personal definition of happiness includes the following:

- *Enjoying my own company.*

- *Being grateful for what I have, rather than complaining about what I don't have.*

- *Taking nothing for granted.*

- *Participating in life and helping others.*

- *Developing new interests.*

- *Feeling passionate about my life's work, which adds meaning to my life.*

- *Having love in my life. Surrounding myself with loving family and friends.*

- *Not waiting for someone else to make me happy. (What a crazy idea anyway!)*

- *Associating with people who have a sense of well-being about themselves. They're already happy and they tend to think in positive ways.*

- *Maintaining and increasing my sense of humor. (Think about how you feel after you've had a good laugh. You might describe it as feeling elated, exhilarated, or even **happy**!)*

- *Appreciating the small things in life such as a beautiful flower, being in nature, hearing the sound of a child's laughter, eating an ice cream cone, or seeing a rainbow.*

Is there a preset level of happiness that is determined by genetics? Psychologists are investigating how the biology of our brains relates to happiness. Recent studies show that identical twins share the same disposition whether they grow up together or not. In an *ABC News Special*, "The Mystery of Happiness: Who Has It…How to Get It," Dr. Richard Davidson, a psychologist at the University of Wisconsin, said, "There are certain brains that are more predisposed to experience happiness compared to other brains." Tests are being done on newborns as early as two days after birth. Findings show that babies who smile a lot have more activity in the left frontal area of the brain, which indicates that they're happier.

Davidson observed this brain activity using a brain imaging device that illuminates the area of the brain that is most active when the subject is experiencing happiness. So it seems to prove that we may be born with a predisposition for being happy—according to Davidson, at least a fifty percent effect of genetic influence. According to Dr. Thomas Bouchard, a psychologist at the University of Minnesota who has done extensive studies on twins, "If only environment shaped our personality, identical twins reared apart would have no similarity, and yet they're every bit as similar as identical twins reared together."

We can't overlook the fact that genetics may play a part in one's predisposition for happiness. If you're not happy, your genes may be partially responsible. Wait a minute! I can hear a lot of you saying, "It's not my fault I'm not happy. I was born genetically challenged—congenitally unhappy. There's nothing I can do to change it!" Don't think you need a gene transplant. Instead, remember that genetics only plays a fifty percent part in your happiness. You CAN change and be happy. But first you must define what happiness means to YOU!

Treat Yourself Gently When Life Throws You a Curve

Unhappiness is in not knowing what we want and killing ourselves to get it.

–Don Herold

The U-turns of happiness. Sometimes life has a way of taking a good feeling and suddenly turning it upside down. For example, did you ever wake up feeling great, only to have your joyous mood unexpectedly change to one of gloom and doom? You try to figure out why. Then you remember the early morning phone call from your "Woe is me" friend who constantly complains about life and loves swimming in their pool of negativity. Your life was fine until you answered the phone. Before you realize it, you become short-tempered and angry at every little thing and everyone. You're no doubt experiencing what I call one of the U-turns of happiness.

Whenever your mood changes for the worst, think of what happened immediately before you started to feel bad. Retrace your mental thoughts. What were you thinking about right before your mood started to change? Dig into your happiness kit, put on your detective hat, and look for clues. If you talked to someone on the phone like the victimized friend above or someone who told you unfortunate news, that can be enough of a reason to change your sunny blue skies to gloom and doom.

Another U-turn some people make on their journey is when they desire things they don't have. Why not enjoy and appreciate what you do have for a change? What's the point of living in your cozy home and always wishing you lived in a mansion? What's the point of driving around in a Volkswagen and feeling miserable whenever a Ferrari passes you? This only makes you unhappy. You'll feel a lot better if you embrace the idea that the best car to drive is the car you're driving at that moment, and the best place to live is where you live now. Ask yourself, "Do I want to feel bitter or better?"

Be forewarned. The list of U-turns goes on and on. They can blind-side you. There are signs you might want to watch for and pay special attention to when you're going along your merry way feeling fine and then all of a sudden you feel unhappy. The following are just a few of them:

Be cautious about comparing yourself to others. It's normal for people to make the mistake of comparing themselves to others and seeing how they come up short. If we take out our mental tape measure, it seems the other person has a better life than we do.

- Don't allow another person's bad mood to influence your disposition.

- If someone tells you some bad news, you can be compassionate, but don't let their bad news bury you.

- Guilt of any kind can often put you in a state of despair. Remember, YOU deserve to be happy and to have goodness in your life.

- Rejection—real or imagined—taps into your insecurities and undoubtedly throws you a curve. Look at it objectively and don't let the situation get out of hand. You won't please everyone all the time.

- Taking things too personally can also be detrimental to your well-being. Even minor incidents, such as a car cutting you off, can be taken too much to heart. Keep things in perspective!

- Visual reminders of the past might make you feel sad. For example, if you broke up with your boyfriend or girlfriend a short while ago, and every time you pass the restaurant where you said your last good-bye it reminds you of him or her, try taking a different route on your way to the office.

Naturally, there are many times when life throws you a curve and you lose your footing. Most people are not happy all the time. Losses occur and bad stuff can happen. Even when a serious tragedy takes place, as it did with my student, Marty Rubinstein, happiness can eventually return in one's life. This is his story:

Nine years ago, a terrible tragedy entered into my life. My wonderful twenty-seven-year-old daughter took her life. She had been living in Albuquerque, New Mexico; I was residing in Santa Barbara, California, at the time. I had been on a business trip to Albuquerque four weeks before this happened and spent some time with Lynn. She seemed fine. So the shock of this tragic act of desperation was almost more than I could bear. When I went back to Albuquerque for Lynn's funeral, I was able to talk to friends and my two sons. It seems that Lynn was experiencing manic-depressive episodes. Her mother, my ex-wife, had been a manic-depressive over the thirty-six years of our marriage, going in and out of mental hospitals every three years. Lynn inherited this terrible disease.

Unless you're with a person on a day-to-day basis, it's easy to miss seeing the symptoms. Lynn certainly fooled me. Needless to say, like any parent, I felt some blame for her suicide. During the memorial service, I tried addressing her "self-death," as I called it during my eulogy. I said that she didn't want to travel through the caverns of the absurd anymore, as this was the way she viewed life. She didn't want to experience what her mother went through all those years.

I think my healing, my going from extreme unhappiness to happiness, may have started when I said those words at Lynn's memorial service. I came back to Santa Barbara, and with a lot of patience, praying, and meditation, eventually became happy again. This is not to say that I don't grieve for my daughter; on her birthday and on the anniversary of her death, I remember her very intensely. But life goes on.

Yes, the good news is that the sun will come up tomorrow. Day follows night. No matter what your current circumstances are, you can heal. Take time to nurture yourself by asking for support from friends, or you may want to seek professional help. Healing takes time, so in the meantime, be kind to yourself.

Make Room for Happiness

*Happiness is something that comes into our lives through doors
we don't even remember leaving open.*

–Rose Lane

*Let go of all the stuff that holds you back from the happiness
you deserve.* To create happiness in your life, you must make
room for it. Imagine the following scenario:

You've decided to buy some new clothes. Perhaps you're starting a new job and you want to improve your professional
image. Or you may have gained or lost weight and your old
clothes no longer fit. Or maybe you've moved to a different cli-
mate and your present wardrobe isn't right. Whatever the reason, you head out to your favorite department store or boutique and purchase several outfits.

When you get home, you realize that your closet is so stuffed
with old clothes that there's no room for one more thing. What
can you do? You could start a new closet somewhere else in the
house, or hang your new clothes on a hook on the back of your
bedroom door (my personal favorite). You might even just

leave your purchases in their original bags to clutter up the room. There are other alternatives I'm sure you can think of, but the best thing to do is to make room for them in your present closet.

To make room for your new clothes, you might begin by trying on everything you own so that you can discard what you don't want. In the process, you make a pile of stuff that doesn't work for you any longer. You get rid of the real mistakes—like the items with the price tags still on them, for instance. You say good-bye to the things that are too tight or no longer comfortable. You even throw out some of your sentimental favorites. Pretty soon you've made room for your new purchases. Proudly, you hang them in your closet and think to yourself: "I'm so GLAD I got rid of that stuff. Why didn't I do it sooner? I feel wonderful!" There's something tremendously cathartic about getting rid of old things.

Like this scenario, there needs to be enough space in your life for happiness to exist and flourish. Many people have their lives cluttered with "stuff." You may be holding on to an unhappy childhood memory that makes you feel miserable and still has you concentrating on what's lacking in your life rather than what's positive about it. You need to realize that you can never go back to that age and its circumstances, so the best thing to do is to forgive yourself and others and move on. This will create space in your life for happiness.

What do you need to let go of before you can become happy?
Here's a quick quiz that will help you sort out your inner closet of old emotional debris.

Do you hold on to **old hurts**? Suppose you were always made
fun of by other children when you were growing up. Your class-
mates teased you and didn't include you in any of their outside
activities. You weren't invited to birthday parties, and you were
the last one to be chosen as a player on athletic teams. No one
wanted to sit next to you in the lunch room. This may have
caused you to feel lonely, hurt, and rejected. Subsequently, you
went through your entire high school years feeling like you did-
n't fit in. These feelings from the past will carry on in your life if
you don't resolve them. First, before you move on, you need to
realize that these feelings come from your *past* and have nothing
to do with the person you are now.

Do you hold on to **anger**? The more anger you hold on to, the
greater your chances of becoming mentally or physically ill,
because anger festers and eats away at you.

Do you hold on to **past resentments**? Perhaps you want
revenge for someone who "did you wrong," and all you can
think about is how to get even. But I ask you, at what price?
What lengths will you go to avenge this wrong? Will you sacri-
fice your own self-worth to get even? Resentment is a heavy

burden to carry around. Chances are, while you're plotting your precious scheme against that person, they're off on vacation in the south of France—being very happy and totally unaware of the vengefulness and vindictive behavior that's doing you mental and physical harm. Instead, you could be making your own reservations for a trip to France.

Do you hold on to **relationships** that no longer serve you well? Perhaps you're involved with people who aren't good for you emotionally. These are the kind of people who constantly point out your shortcomings or humiliate you in front of other friends. They don't remember what important thing you told them yesterday. Spending time with them may be holding you back from improving yourself. Be courageous and go it alone for a while. Stop seeing people who don't have your best interests at heart.

Now that you've cleaned out the clutter of your closet with your mental broom, you can allow for new creativity and healthy relationships to enter into your life. You'll feel liberated and free of the excess baggage that's been holding you back. You can now look forward to going out and doing more of what works in your life and makes you happy.

5

Forgive Yourself and Others

Don't carry a grudge. While you're carrying the grudge, the other guy's out dancing.

–Buddy Hackett

Dance the dance of forgiveness . . . one step at a time! If your dance card is filled with resentment, but your dance partner with whom you're angry is in sync with the rhythm and having a good time, it's obvious that your hostility is wasted. You may want your partner to be miserable, and you think the way to accomplish this is to punish them. But you're just hurting yourself, so why not practice the four steps to forgiveness instead? Forgiving can be difficult, especially when you've been hurt. Here's what you can do to begin the process of forgiveness:

Recognize that it's best for YOU to forgive. Say to yourself, "I forgive myself. I give myself permission to move on with my life and be happy." Repeat this affirmation as often as possible.

Part of the difficulty in forgiving is that you're usually angry. Recognize that behind anger there's sadness and hurt. When you're angry, ask yourself, "What am I feeling sad about?"

Give yourself time. You don't have to forgive everything and everyone all at once. It's okay to go from being very angry at someone to gradually forgiving them.

Realize that you're not perfect, and neither is anyone else. You'll make mistakes in life as everyone else does. But you still have a choice. Once you forgive, you're free. You're no longer pre-occupied with the person you were angry with.

Remember, to forgive doesn't mean to forget. If you forget why you were angry or hurt, you're more apt to make the same mistake in the future. Take this example: You've lent money to a friend. They don't repay the loan. You notice they're driving a new car and you still haven't been paid. You mention this to them and they say, "Oh gosh, I'm sorry. I'll get to it right away." After a few months, your friend has the audacity to ask you for another loan. You wonder if "patsy" is written across your forehead. You express your anger at not having been paid for the first loan. An argument ensues, and both of you leave mad. You feel betrayed, hurt, and angry. This person is occupying too much space in your mind, so you need to forgive them and move on. Once you do this, you can be rid of this person. There's no need for ill will.

When you can forgive yourself and others, you develop internal freedom. You can add happiness to your life and gain peace of mind. You won't feel contented if you're holding on to a lot of resentment. As Louise Hay writes in her book *The Power Is Within You,* "When we forgive and let go, not only does a huge weight drop off our shoulders, but the doorway to our own self-love opens up."

Come on, get out on the dance floor. Get in step. Get out there and slow dance your way to forgiveness.

6

If You Must Be a Critic, Give Yourself Rave Reviews

Pay no attention to what the critics say; there has never been set up a statue in honor of a critic.

–Jean Sibelius

Do away with "self put-down" behavior. If you choose to belittle yourself all the time, it's hard for you to see what you do well. It's like wearing a pair of fogged-up glasses. Cleaning your glasses of self-criticism enables you to like yourself. You can then start doing more of what works in your life because you can finally see your strengths and talents.

My great-grandmother used to say, "No one can do to you what you do to yourself." As a young girl, I had no idea what she was talking about. I later understood this to mean that no one can be as critical and judge you as harshly as you judge yourself.

Much of the time, we're nicer to strangers than we are to ourselves. Have you ever been out window shopping, not looking where you were going, and you bumped into someone accidentally? What was your reaction? Did you say to the person,

"Excuse me. I'm sorry. Are you okay?" At the same time, were you thinking to yourself, "What a stupid klutz I am. Why didn't I look before I turned around and started walking?"

When you begin to pay attention to your reactions in situations like these, you may find that this self put-down behavior filters into many areas of your life. If you'd like to make an immediate, positive change in your life, promise to stop criticizing yourself. To do this, look inside your happiness kit for these three tools:

1. *Be aware that you may be more critical of yourself than anyone else is.*

2. *Listen to your self-talk. Watch the self name-calling.*

3. *When you notice your critical voice talking, interrupt it, pat yourself on the back and say, "That's okay. Thanks for sharing." Then move on.*

If you're angry with yourself for being self-critical, have patience. Your inner dialogue will change the more you use these tools. To change critical behavior, repeat the new behavior of being kind to yourself. Treat yourself as an honored guest in your daily routine. For example, if you use your best china and silver only for guests, why not change that habit and use it for yourself as well?

Turn a criticism into a positivism. Learn to approve of yourself. Develop compassion toward yourself. Concentrate on your strengths. What do you like about yourself? Make a "What's Good About Me" list. Each day, try adding one thing to it. If you don't add to the list, review it and think about one of the positivisms you already have on the list. For example, your list might look something like this:

* *I may be shy, but I'm a good listener.*

* *I'm not a gourmet cook, but I bake a great chocolate cake.*

* *My housekeeping skills leave something to be desired, but I get great satisfaction from making my bed every day.*

Keep it simple. The idea is to refocus your mind and thoughts —**focus on what's right with you rather than what's wrong with you.** Just imagine the difference it would make if a parent reproached a child by saying, "Johnny, what is right with you?" instead of yelling, "Johnny, what is wrong with you?" This alone could change the way Johnny feels about himself.

Practice kindness toward yourself; give yourself rave reviews. Realize you're doing the best you can do. When you're less critical of yourself, something magical happens. You're also less critical of others. Therefore, you'll have better relationships. Adopt this idea and apply it often: **I treat myself as an honored guest each and every day.**

7

Look Inside Yourself
for Happiness

Your success and happiness lie in you.

–Helen Keller

Happiness is in your own backyard! Your journey to happiness starts from within you. It's how you feel about yourself that adds to or detracts from your personal happiness. You already have everything inside you to make yourself happy. It may just be that your innate happiness has gotten dusty with old beliefs and past feelings such as thinking you have no one who believes in you, or no matter what you do, you're not good enough. **You ARE good enough just the way you are.** Don't forget this. Make "I Am Good Enough" a daily affirmation.

Also, you may have a trunk load of guilt that has manifested itself in your belief that you don't deserve happiness. Happiness is a natural state that you already possess, and you may only need to find your way back. A client of mine tells this story of how he found the happiness he so rightfully deserved.

I had always wanted to be a firefighter, but my family and friends wanted me to take over the family retail clothing

business. I did that for a couple of years and I was miserable and developed an ulcer. I landed up in the hospital where I began to reexamine my life. I started listening to my inner voice. As a child, firemen had been my heroes. I was always in awe of the way they saved lives. So I became a fireman and I'm happy that I found the courage to finally follow my dream. **My philosophy is, Go within to find happiness. Don't look for it in an aftershave or a Maidenform bra where they promise you superficial happiness. You must go within. It can be difficult, but I've found happiness within myself by having a positive attitude and taking charge of my own life.**

As the above story illustrates, even if you feel you've never been happy, it's not too late for you to become happy.

Take charge of your life. It gives you the energy to create the time you need to enjoy the pleasures of life. When you take charge of your life, you feel that you're in control of your destiny. You don't wait for things to happen, you make things happen, and this makes you feel good. You're no longer merely a spectator in your life but an active participant, and whenever you participate in life, it brings happiness and fulfillment.

Does happiness seem to elude you? Have you been searching for happiness, but the harder you look, the harder it is to find?

The fact is, the more you're trying to be happy, the more elusive it can become.

Happiness is not exactly tangible. It's more like the liquid bubbles you blew as a child—the kind that come in a jar with a plastic wand that has a loop on the end of it. After you blew a great bubble, you'd try to catch it, but as soon as you touched it, it disappeared. So you'd blow another one and just let it glide along until it hit an object or the ground—and poof! It was gone, too.

Ask children what fascinates them about these bubbles and they might tell you that it's the way they just float in the air or how they vanish into thin air. Think of happiness as a bubble. It's ethereal, and when you try too hard to capture it, it evaporates.

Are you looking for happiness in all the wrong places? There ought to be a placard that reads, "Don't Look Here for Happiness," when we get to those places. Stop trying so hard to be happy. Become aware of the inappropriate areas where you might be seeking happiness. If you're looking for it in any of the following areas, you might want to reevaluate your search.

Money. The idea that money will solve all your problems and bring you supreme happiness is a myth. There are plenty of wealthy people who are depressed. (I can hear some of you objecting, "But if I'm not happy, I might as well be rich!") You

Happiness Instruction Kit

need to look no further than to some of the celebrated people of our time (e.g., the Getty family, famous rock stars, and others who commit suicide, etc.).

Fame and power. Many people who have obtained both don't describe themselves as happy. For them, it never seems to be enough or it doesn't last. Many say they feel insecure because they think people love them only to be close to power and fame, not for who they are.

Relationships. Looking to another person to make you happy is always the wrong place to look. Others may enhance your happiness or add to it, **but no other person can make you happy.** (This is good news—for if no one can make you happy, then no one can make you unhappy either.) Unfortunately, we're influenced to think otherwise, through the love songs we hear, poetry we read, movies we see, and even the classic love stories we've come to cherish. They all convey the feeling that alone, by ourselves, we're not complete.

Singles bars. Sexual conquests are another way of seeking happiness. It's an antidote only for a short period of time and you may feel worse later.

Vacations. Perhaps you think that getting away from it all to an exotic island will make your life perfect. Think again. You take yourself with you, so if you're miserable at home, guess what—it won't get any better in Bora Bora.

Shopping. "When the going gets tough, the tough go shopping." Acquiring things never brings enduring happiness. It's merely a quick fix. And you have to keep shopping for new things to give you that instant rush.

Food. Many people seek food to comfort themselves. Overeating works for a few moments, but guilt usually sets in after the whole box of chocolates, and it overrides any sense of happiness. You start to hate yourself and go for the second box. This becomes a never-ending cycle.

Mind-altering substances. Drugs and alcohol may numb you temporarily, but they only lead to further unhappiness and depression or worse.

Marriage. If only you'd meet the right person and get married, then you'd surely be happy. If this is what you think, the honeymoon won't last long. Some of you may have tried this over and over.

Only you can provide the peace of mind, contentment, and happiness that you so deserve. It's exhilarating and liberating to think that you don't need to rely on anyone else to bring you happiness. It's been with you all along, inside you, ready and waiting for you to feel worthy of it. Like a pair of glasses you thought you'd misplaced, only to discover them right there on top of your head, happiness is right there with you.

8

Be Grateful for What You Have in Life

We tend to forget that happiness doesn't come as a result of getting something we don't have, but rather of recognizing and appreciating what we do have.

–Frederick Koenig

When life deals you lemons, make lemonade! My mother was the best lemonade maker I ever knew. She made a lot of lemonade in her lifetime. She always taught me to look for the best in a situation and to look for the good in myself, which reminds me of another of her favorite expressions, "Get the good out of it." It didn't matter what IT was. Even to this day, I concentrate on what's working in my life. Each day when I awake, I think of one good thing I'm grateful for. **Your first thought when you awaken in the morning sets the mood for your entire day.** So rather than waking up and hitting the snooze button so you can go back to sleep for an extra ten minutes, why not sleep the extra ten minutes first, then wake up and start your day with a positive thought?

My mother suffered for many years with emphysema. She died

in 1994. I saw how difficult her life was and often wondered how she maintained such a positive attitude. She told me that she didn't dwell on her illness and was grateful for all that she had in spite of her affliction. She visualized herself being well every day. Because of her gratitude for life itself, she was able to maintain a positive attitude and live longer than expected.

Think about everything that YOU have to be thankful for in your life. Whether you're young or old, become aware of the importance of being grateful. I marvel at the insight of Ryan Miner, a fifteen-year-old student who wrote the following:

As a young man in today's society, I believe that most people aren't as happy with what they have as they should be. A lot of people take for granted the really important things in life. It took a serious eye injury in my life for me to understand how important having a family and being healthy are. So to those of you who are striving to find true happiness, stop and take a moment to look at what you do have rather than what you don't have.

At the other end of the age spectrum is Martha Mullins, ninety-eight years old, who said:

My life has not always been easy. I have suffered many losses, which caused me to face many things and brought about much self-growth. I realized the importance of staying

active and being with people. I am active in the Red Cross and in many environmental issues in the community. I am also a mentor to elementary school children. They keep me young. I have not withdrawn from life in the least.

Start your very own J.A.G.—Journal of Appreciation & Gratitude. Set aside some time. Write down what you appreciate about yourself and what you're grateful for. You'd be surprised at what writing things down every day will do for you. An older woman in one of my seminars told me that she took herself completely for granted until she began to write down what she appreciated about herself each day. She was shocked to discover how meaningful her life really was, and she has since developed a new respect for herself and all that she does.

After a week or so of keeping your journal, if you've written down each day that you're grateful for having a roof over your head, then you'll appreciate the fact that your roof doesn't leak when it rains.

Get started now! You can begin with things like:

Opportunities you've experienced such as learning about yourself through relationships and your career as well as other chances for personal growth and development.

Events like birthdays, anniversaries, job promotions,

> *educational accomplishments, family reunions, etc., that have shaped your life.*

> *People who enhanced your life or added to your happiness, such as your grandparents, parents, mentors, friends, and acquaintances.*

All these ideas make your journal a personal self-history.

There are so many things we take for granted. Think of when you cut your finger and had a bandage on it. You were surprised at how much you used that finger. It wasn't until something happened to it that you were aware of how much you needed it. Have you ever lost electricity and been frustrated because you didn't have light, you didn't have access to your computer, your freezer had shut off, and you couldn't cook on your electric stove? You've developed new respect for Thomas Edison. Don't wait for something to break to be grateful.

First and foremost, develop an attitude of gratitude and appreciation for the most important person in your life, YOU. Thank yourself and give yourself credit for all you do during the day.

9

Don't Wait Around for Happiness to Happen

Happiness is not something you postpone for the future; it is something you design for the present.

–Jim Rohn

Let's play the "waiting game." Think of a time when you had to wait for something. For example, have you ever experienced an endless wait at a restaurant where you were meeting a friend for dinner? You arrived at the agreed upon time—and you waited. You ordered an appetizer and finished it. You kept looking at your watch and the people waiting for tables and giving excuses to the waiter for your friend's tardiness. Fairly soon, you began to second-guess yourself, thinking you had the wrong time or even the wrong day of the week. By the time your friend showed up, you were so angry you couldn't enjoy the dinner.

Maybe you've waited a long time in line at the supermarket, and just as you were about to load your items on the conveyor, the checkout person posted a sign reading "Aisle Closed." Or perhaps, while waiting in your doctor's office, you had time to read an entire *Reader's Digest* and become all too familiar with the photo layouts in *People* magazine. You were ready to get up and leave when the receptionist called your name for your appointment. She directed you to a sterile cubicle where you waited another indefinite amount of time. You were instructed to put on a crisp paper gown (you know, the ones that fit two-dimensional people). Finally, the doctor arrived and told you how sorry he or she was for keeping you waiting. Inside, you were seething, but you didn't express your irritation.

Why do we become angry in these situations? It's simple. When you wait for something, you feel powerless, and when you feel powerless, anger is quick to follow. Waiting is a passive state that takes away the feeling of being in control of yourself. You never know if you're going to get the result you're waiting for or when it'll happen. You're in limbo. This not knowing is what causes you anxiety.

It's good to be aware of the tentative emotional state you put yourself in when you wait. If you're waiting an unreasonable amount of time for someone, you may think the person you're waiting for has no regard for your time. This may or may not be true. You might begin to feel unimportant. It's easy to personalize things when you're waiting.

If you find yourself in the waiting game, the most important thing to remember is that you have options. For example, you can call the person you're waiting for and leave a message that you had to leave. In the case of the doctor, you might phone ahead of time to see if he or she is on schedule. If they're still way behind when you get there, don't be afraid to tell them you're annoyed at having waited so long. When you take control of a situation, you give back power to yourself.

What needs to happen for happiness to show up in your life?
Maybe you're waiting to reach a certain age before you're happy. Research has shown that "people at every age are about, on average, equally happy. . . . People in their 20s, 30s, 60s, 70s report the same levels of happiness." These facts were disclosed on the *ABC News Special*, "The Mystery of Happiness: Who Has It . . . How to Get It." Furthermore, it's a myth to think that as you age, you become less happy. "As we age . . . our highs become less high, but the lows are also less low, because we learn to accept the things we can't change. Older people often describe their lives as hard, but they also say they feel less stress. And so, older people report happiness levels just as high as the young," the program explained.

Don't put yourself in a holding pattern like an airline pilot who's ready to land at the destination but must circle and wait. Quit circling happiness; it's time to land. Seize every opportunity— and there are many—to live life to its fullest and allow happiness into your life.

DON'T WAIT for the "perfect" mate to magically show up in your life. Get out there and find him or her. As a friend once said to me, "Willa, the only man you'll ever meet by staying home is, maybe, the fireman."

DON'T WAIT for the "right time" to take that vacation. Take it sooner rather than later.

DON'T WAIT for a new job to fall into your lap. Find out what's available and go after it. Be persistent and call back, and back, and back again. At least you'll be on a first-name basis with the secretary.

DON'T WAIT to increase your awareness of your gratitude for simple events such as sunrises and sunsets, the magnificence of trees and flowers. As Georgia O'Keefe said, "If you take a flower in your hand and really look at it, it's your world for the moment." So appreciate your world.

DON'T WAIT..., for as Ken Keyes says in his book *Prescriptions for Happiness,* "Postponed happiness may be lost happiness."

Clone a Happy
Attitude

*Words can never adequately convey the incredible impact of our
attitude toward life. The longer I live the more convinced I become
that life is ten percent what happens to us and ninety percent
how we respond to it.*

–Charles R. Swindoll

If you want to be happy for a lifetime, change your attitude! I
love the above quote. I have it posted in my office where I can
see it easily. It serves as a reminder that I have a choice regarding my reactions to situations, and that things are never as bad
as they seem. It always lifts my spirits.

I first saw this quote in a rehabilitation hospital where people
who have had traumatic accidents and suffered brain damage
and strokes are cared for. Many of them are in wheelchairs and
have endured great physical and emotional loss. Yet, many
were quite happy. To me it proves the point that "life is ten percent what happens to us and ninety percent how we respond
to it."

There are many times in life when our spirits need lifting and we need to keep a positive attitude. For example, on a trip to Pittsburgh, I met Evelyn, whose positive attitude helped her survive a life-threatening illness and eventually brought happiness into her life again. This is her story:

After the death of my first husband, I realized even more how important a positive attitude is. This became even more obvious when a year later I was diagnosed with breast cancer. I got through chemotherapy, surgery, and reconstruction with the loving support of family and friends as well as very caring medical professionals. My employer allowed me sufficient time to recover and never made me feel that my job was in jeopardy.

Years later, I am cancer free, happily married to a wonderful gentleman, and enjoying a new extended family including two grandsons, ages four and seven. There is no doubt that a positive mental attitude and the love and support of family and friends have brought me to this place and time in my life.

Your attitude affects your response to whatever happens to you. It's largely a reflection of whether you invite happiness into your life or you make it difficult to experience happiness. Many people feel they're powerless when it comes to changing their attitudes. This is not true. If you need an attitude adjustment, with a little inspiration you can do it yourself.

This brings to mind a friend who hates to get a parking ticket. To deal with her angry attitude, when she gets a ticket, she turns it into a positive experience by telling herself, "Good, I'll send in a check to keep the city looking beautiful with fountains, flowers, and maintenance of our lovely city parks. I'm happy to do it!"

Become a happychondriac by taking out some more tools from your happiness kit.

Get an attitude transplant. If you could truly do this, whose attitude would you want? I personally would want Mitchell's. At a young age, he was in a terrible motorcycle accident and burned beyond recognition. Four years later, he was in an airplane crash, which paralyzed him from the waist down. Today Mitchell is a respected public speaker and a successful business person. His attitude is, "It's not what happens to you, it's what you do about it." He never asks, "Why me?" or feels sorry for himself. There are always plenty of good attitudes to go around. And cloning a happy attitude is an outpatient procedure with immediate results.

Fill an imaginary pitcher with happiness. When it comes to attitude and one's level of happiness in life, aren't you tired of people talking about seeing the pitcher half empty or half full?

Start a new trend and look at your pitcher as always being full. After all, isn't life a cup to be filled and not drained? Look at your life as full and filled with happiness. After all, the Bible doesn't say, "My cup runneth out."

Surround yourself with people who have a lot of interests. I'm inspired by people who have many interests. These people are stimulating and have enthusiasm about life. Being around them can lift your spirits.

Write down all the things that influence your attitude. This will make you aware of your present attitude and how much it's affected by things you may not even be aware of. Consider the following when making your list. You can use it as a guide.

- *Health*
- *Self-esteem*
- *Sleep, too much or too little*
- *Love and friendship*
- *Money*
- *Work*
- *Exercise*
- *Emotions*

Weather

 Diet

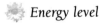 *Energy level*

Still need some happiness help? Try filling one of Willa's happiness prescriptions:

Twice a day, take a dose of appreciation of yourself. Stop judging yourself so much. Think of two things you're good at or you've accomplished. Do more of those things.

Call yourself sometime during the day and leave a positive message on your answering machine. Tell yourself you're great. When you get home and check your messages, you'll be smiling!

Before bedtime, take a dose of gratitude for the good things you have in your life. Reflect on the day and think about things you're grateful for. Even if you simply made it through a difficult day, be grateful you made it through.

Give yourself a break every day. Go easy on yourself. Concentrate each day on one way you improved your attitude. Keep it simple. You always have a choice of what your attitude can be in any given situation. Remind

yourself of what you did right. Say to yourself, "I'm okay,"
and tell everyone, "I'm a happychondriac and I'm proud
of it."

Get Your Past out
of Your Present

People are just about as happy as they make up their minds to be.

–Abraham Lincoln

You are what you think you are. A beginning step to becoming a happier person is to start changing negative thoughts and beliefs you have about yourself. Ask yourself, "Where does the negativity I feel about myself come from?" The answer is that it's the result of all your past experience, including what others such as parents and teachers have told you about yourself. As a child, you believed a lot of what you were told—things that may not have been true. As an adult, you may be hanging on to those false beliefs about yourself and the world.

For example, if you got the idea from your parents (who may have had a miserable life) that life is a struggle and no one deserves to be happy, then you may feel that your life should be miserable, too. If your parents were unhappy, you may feel guilty about living a happier life than they did. To explore your thoughts about yourself, you have to become more aware of your thought processes and beliefs about yourself. Acknowledge and accept your thoughts and feelings about yourself, without being judgmental, and begin to examine them. Ask yourself, "Is the way I think about myself right for me TODAY?" If not, start with the present and notice how your past beliefs are no longer appropriate in your life now.

You only do yourself injustice by not understanding your own thought process. In his book *You Can Be Happy No Matter What*, Richard Carlson tells us that "because our thought systems are filled with our memory of the past, information we have accumulated throughout our lifetimes, they encourage us to see things in the same way. We react negatively (or positively) to the same circumstances over and over again, interpreting our own experiences in life as we have in the past."

In one of my seminars on happiness, a young woman, Jennifer Coates, shared the following:

When I look back on my childhood, I think fun and happiness were discouraged in my family. I remember my sister and I, who generally didn't play together, having a great time one night. We were laughing and acting silly in front of some guests. My father made us stop, yelling "That's enough now," giving us the message that when we laughed or got excited or even felt "happy," it was wrong to feel that way. I never remember having a good time without this kind of reprimand. I think my dad is uncomfortable with intense or

strong emotions of all kinds. I can never even remember being hugged by my dad. Too bad.

As an adult, Jennifer came to realize how much her past family beliefs prevented her from enjoying her life. It was time for her to shed herself of the beliefs she had learned from childhood and establish her own beliefs.

You may still be wearing some of the clothes from your childhood closet. Do you walk around with a general feeling of discomfort, as though you were wearing someone else's clothes? Naturally, they don't fit so well any longer. Things have gotten a little tight around the waist and the pants are shorter than you remembered. But you're still trying to somehow make them fit. This may account for the feeling you have that you're someone other than the person whose life you're **acting out.** This is key. Many people are simply acting out what others believed about them or told them.

A belief is only a thought. Some people think a thought is only a thought, but our thoughts have as much power as we give them. If you're unhappy, chances are you're not having good thoughts about yourself. The thoughts you have and how you think about yourself have a lot to do with how you feel.

When I was a child, my mother would say, "You are what you think you are." When I asked her what that meant, she replied,

"It's simple. If you think you're great, you will be great. If you think you're so-so, then that's what you'll be." To illustrate her point, she used an example of someone I knew from school. "Look at Nelsa," she would say, "you can tell she thinks she's great just by the way she walks." Over the years, I found her simple words to be quite true. *You are what you think you are.*

A person once asked me, "Well, if I really don't think I'm great, should I just pretend I am?" I replied, "Yes! If you pretend you're great, you'll start to act the way great people act, you'll gain self-confidence and begin to believe you're unique and special. **Repeating this new behavior helps you believe it and you will feel comfortable and, eventually, you'll change how you think about yourself.**" It's kind of like a new pair of shoes: the more you wear them, the more comfortable they become and the happier you'll be.

Don't think of happiness as a special gift bestowed on just a few. You deserve to be happy, even if no one around you is. This includes family and friends. You deserve it just because you're you; there is no one exactly like you in the world, and the past IS the past. Get your past out of your present and be happy now!

Watch Your Expectations

*The more reasonable we are in our expectations,
the fewer disappointments we will have in life.*

–A. Nielen

Do you have a lot of unrealistic expectations about relationships and events in your life? At a party, I overheard some men and women talking about their mates. The conversation turned to expectations of what their mates should do. One woman said, "I have only one expectation of my husband." I eagerly awaited her answer. She said, "I only expect him to breathe." Everyone laughed, but she was serious. Later, when I reflected on her remark, I thought she had touched upon something important—the fact that many of us have unrealistic expectations in life, particularly of other people fulfilling our every dream.

Having high expectations can set you up for disappointment—even in small ways. Everyone has been to a movie or a play that they thought would be great because it was highly recommended, only to be disappointed by it. The performance didn't measure up to what their expectations were.

You may have had similar experiences with vacations and restaurants. You enjoyed yourself, but wondered what all the fuss was about. At some point, after many of these kinds of disappointments, you may begin to realize that you've developed a pattern in your life—to overanticipate and at times actually visualize your whole experience before you leave home. For example, many people visualize their vacation before they even leave home—everything from the hotel they'll be staying in to the various restaurants they hope to find. I think everyone does this to a certain extent. I've even done it with blind dates! So the question is, How do you lead your life to avoid setting yourself up for disappointment? **Watch your expectations. Are they realistic?** For example, you can't expect to take one class in French, fly to Paris, and speak the language fluently when you get there.

Warning! Be careful. Your life will be happier when you have realistic expectations. Live one day at time. That's all that's possible.

Eliminate the Limitations You Place on Your Happiness

*Many people think that if they were only in some other place,
or had some other job, they would be happy. Well, that is doubtful.
So get as much happiness out of what you are doing as you can
and don't put off being happy until some future date.*

–Dale Carnegie

If only's—and woulda, shoulda, coulda's. "I would be happy if only _____." Take a moment and finish this sentence. Fill in whatever comes to mind. Whatever it is, it's a requirement that restricts you from becoming a happy person. How many times have you caught yourself saying, "I would be happy if only

* *I had a good relationship."*

* *I had a lot more money."*

* *I had more time."*

* *I had a better job."*

* *I had a lot of friends."*

I won the lottery."

I didn't have so much responsibility."

I was more attractive."

I had gone to college."

I lost twenty pounds."

I wasn't so lonely."

I wasn't so depressed."

I was famous."

I had no worries."

I lived somewhere else."

I was someone else."

Where are *you* placing limitations to your own happiness? Formulate your own "if only—woulda, shoulda, coulda" list. Just remember, many of the "if only's" you'll come up with are common to all of us. The sad truth is that even when you do lose the weight, find a good relationship, or make a lot more money, the happiness doesn't seem to last. A student of mine, Roger, put it this way:

The kind of happiness that I have grown to find most desirable is not the kind that people typically think of what it is

to be happy. While you can find a certain kind of happiness through the enjoyment of particular pleasures such as getting and spending money, eating good food, or anything else that feeds our most basic desires, this is not the kind of long-lasting happiness that will make you most content and most satisfied with your life. Rather, it's through dedication and devotion to common and worthwhile commitments such as volunteering at my local hospital and being a mentor to young people in my community that I find the most gratifying form of happiness.

Happiness is temporary when we get what we desire because too great a value has been placed on it. Then, once our goal is attained, we begin to crave something else that we feel is missing from our lives. We do this because our focus is always on the outside rather than the inside.

When you feel good about yourself, when you develop your self-confidence to the point where you feel you deserve to be happy, then you'll be happy. Make the words "I deserve to be happy" your mantra. Repeat these words over and over again, every chance you get. They help.

So you think winning the lottery will make you happy? It's really interesting and instructive to take a look at lottery winners. Indeed, there must be a period of euphoria when a person wins the lottery. But after the high is over, many winners report that within a year they're no happier than they were before. In fact, lottery winners have a high divorce rate and fewer friends after they win. Some winners report that within three years they've lost all the money in a financial venture or given it away.

In his book *The Pursuit of Happiness*, David Myers cites research indicating that "ordinary activities [the winners] previously enjoyed, such as reading or eating a good breakfast, actually became less pleasurable. Winning the lottery was such an emotional high that, by comparison, their ordinary pleasures paled."

Why don't lottery winners stay happy after they've won? Why do some not even keep the money? After all, they were able to buy whatever they wanted. On the *ABC News Special* "The Mystery of Happiness: Who Has It . . . How to Get It," one lottery winner who was interviewed said, "People have a misconception about having money. You go out and you go, 'Oh, that's what I want, I'll buy it.' Well, a couple of weeks later, . . . that emptiness comes back. Then what?"

After the lottery winners' excitement, disbelief, and elation over winning have subsided, internally they're still the same people. With or without the money, unless they feel good about themselves beforehand, the winnings can't make them feel like worthwhile people. To many, it's a double letdown because they don't feel they deserve the money.

Whatever your "woulda, shoulda, coulda's" are, remember that happiness comes from the inside. You deserve good things in your life, whether it be, yes, winning the lottery, good relationships, or having a career that you love.

You can learn a lot from your "if only's" list. Review your list. Are these "if only's" really necessary? Do you need to carry them around with you as extra baggage on your journey? What action can you take and what solutions can you find to eliminate the limitations you place on your happiness?

As my Uncle Howard says, "Do you want the inscription on your gravestone to read 'Here lies so-and-so. I shoulda and I coulda'? Or do you want it to read 'I did it'?"

Remain Positive–
Avoid the Negativity
Booby Trap

*No man ever injured his eyesight by looking
on the bright side of things.*

–Unknown

Life can be a bowl of cherries. To oversimplify for a moment, there are two kinds of people in the world: the optimist who views life as an adventure, and the pessimist, or fault-finder, who is always stuck in the pits. If you're at the bottom of the pit, you probably need to uncover a few ways to avoid the negativity booby trap.

Artist Shandra Belknap wrote:

If I look at why I'm a happy person, I think the main reason is that I have a positive attitude about everything. My life hasn't always been easy, but I think what has pulled me through the most difficult periods has been a sense of hope and belief in the knowledge that nothing ever stays the same, and that adversity will pass. And no matter how much I may feel sorry for myself at a particularly troubled

time, I'm always able to remember that many people are much worse off, and I become thankful for the blessings I *do* have. That always lifts my spirits. And suddenly what I don't have doesn't seem all that terrible anymore.

If you want to be a person who's filled with hope and optimism instead of always being afraid that the sky is falling, check out what's in your happiness kit. In there, you'll find many tools you can use to stay out of the pits. Try them out and see what works for you. They might include some of the following:

Thirty Tools for Keeping a Positive Attitude

Don't complain for more than two minutes at a time.

Stay away from other people who complain more than one minute at a time.

Do one good deed for someone other than yourself every day.

Eat plenty of chocolate.

Laugh often.

Listen to your feelings.

Stay out of other people's affairs, unless you're invited in.

Go to a card shop and read the humorous cards.

Sing in the shower or in your car. Just sing.

Smile. Did you know it takes twenty-six muscles to smile and sixty-two muscles to frown?

Take a catnap.

Don't "tragicize" by thinking the worst will always happen.

Take a stroll in the park.

Swing on a swing.

Take an aromatherapy bath.

Fly a kite.

Walk barefoot on the beach.

Count all the stars in sight on a starry night.

When you make a mistake, forgive yourself.

Be flexible. Go with the flow.

Read a favorite book.

Don't say "yes" when you really want to say "no" to something.

Forget about being right all the time. Give someone else a chance.

Give yourself a pep talk.

Give hugs freely.

When you feel rejected, don't take it personally.

Give four compliments freely every day. Start with yourself.

Get rid of stuff you don't need or want.

Remember that each day in your life is a new start.

Always look forward, never behind.

If you do find yourself heading toward the pits, you might put aside some time during the day to give yourself a "poor me" party. Set a time limit—ten minutes is plenty. Exaggerate everything that's currently wrong in your life. Give it all you've got. Ask yourself a thousand times, "Why does this always happen to me?" Reaffirm your belief that you were born unlucky. Overindulge in food. Pace back and forth. Worry a lot.

Sometime during your "poor me" party, hopefully you'll realize how absurd this all is and laugh about it. Visualize putting your self-pity in a big garbage bag, throwing it out, and letting go of feeling sorry for yourself. Then at the end of ten minutes, you can be free to go out and celebrate with a "positive me" party.

Fill Your Life with Affirmations

You are today where thoughts have brought you;
you will be tomorrow where your thoughts take you.

–James Allen

It's your thoughts that count! Many people live their lives thinking negative thoughts, and they may not even realize it. If you have a tendency toward negative thinking, try altering your negative thought pattern into a positive one and see what happens! You might ask, "But how do I do that?" One good answer is "By using affirmations." (I call these Happymations!)

What *are* affirmations? Simply put, affirmations are positive statements that help you take control of your thoughts and emotions so you can improve your life. In her book *Revolution From Within*, Gloria Steinem defined affirmations as "the repetition of a phrase with positive personal meaning."

It's so important that your thoughts and words be in tune with what you want. Why on earth would you affirm what you don't want? People do this unconsciously all the time. Consider the phrase "I never have enough time for my own needs." This is a phrase women often use who try to DO IT ALL. By saying this, they unknowingly undermine creating time for their own needs. A more productive phrase might be "I balance my needs with my family's needs."

Affirmation practices have been employed for centuries. Today they remain a powerful method of goal attainment in many areas such as relationships, profession, health, and overall enjoyment of life. Make affirmations an integral and important part of your personal growth. You can benefit greatly by applying affirmations. Use them to

- *Relieve anxiety*
- *Overcome fear*
- *Build confidence*
- *Negate being a victim*
- *Realize your full potential*
- *Take control of your life*

There are three primary ways to perform affirmations. You can repeat empowering expressions aloud, write them down, or use what I call the visual method.

Say it, affirm it, embrace it, and believe it! You can recite and repeat affirmations anywhere, anytime. For example, you could recite and repeat your affirmations immediately upon arising in the morning and again right before you go to bed. I sing my affirmations to any tune that comes into my head. You might try this while you're in the shower, cooking a meal, or driving in your car.

Write your affirmations down. You might jot them down on a 3" x 5" card and carry them with you so you can refer to them often. When you write something, you're apt to give it more credence than the spoken word. In this case, you would write the same thing over and over several times. For instance, if you're trying to lose weight, you might write the phrase "I lose weight easily now."

Use a visual method. Be inventive with your visual affirmations. For example, if you want more money in your life, go out and make enough photocopies of a $100 bill to wallpaper your office. Or you might do as Jim Carey did when he was an unemployed actor. He wrote out a check to himself for $10 million and carried it in his wallet. He was manifesting prosperity into his life. Years later, he received a $10 million check for one of the movies he made. Consider writing out a check to yourself today.

My son, Beaumont, created a wall of frames after he received an award from school for outstanding achievement. He wanted to have it framed, so we went to the frame store. At the framer's, he bought twelve frames. Later in the day, I went into his room and saw all twelve frames hung on the wall above his desk. Eleven were empty. Curious as to why there were eleven empty frames already on the wall, I asked him about it. He informed me matter of factly of all the future awards that would come, and he wanted all the frames to match. This was one of the best examples of a visual affirmation I had ever seen. And it worked! He already has ten of the eleven frames with awards in them.

Begin your pathway to transformation today. Give better quality to thoughts about yourself. An effective, easy way to begin using affirmations is to decide what area of your life you want to work on. Some of these areas might include love, forgiveness, money, career, or physical or mental health. The samples below are just a beginning. The possibilities are endless.

LOVE—Create more love in your relationships

> *"Love enters my life in all that I do."*

> *"I give and accept love freely."*

FORGIVENESS—Forgive and move on

> *"I am free of anger and resentment."*

> *"I choose to forgive and move past the hurt."*

MONEY—Bring more abundance into your life

"Every day, in every way, more prosperity enters my life."

"It's okay to be wealthy and happy."

CAREER—Meet career goals

"My goals are clear."

"I have the job I want."

PHYSICAL HEALTH—Good health affirmations for body image

"I am experiencing good health."

"My body always heals itself."

Affirmations are a good tool for self-help. In your Happiness Instruction Kit, you have a treasure chest of wisdom that challenges you to look at old beliefs that may be causing you unhappiness. You can make up your own affirmations. If you can't easily make up positive statements, go to a bookstore and look at some of the many affirmation books available today. Use affirmations on a daily basis to help you reprogram your thoughts and create the life you want.

16

Be a Passionate, Participating, People Person

Happiness is not an end product in itself. It is a by-product of working, playing, loving, and living.

–Haim Ginott

One weekend I was standing on the sidelines watching my cousin Zack play soccer, a game I don't fully understand. His team roared down the field and everyone started screaming as they anticipated a goal. The ball shot back and forth across the field, always precariously close to falling into the opposing team's control. Then within only a few feet of the goal, the opposing team did capture the ball and suddenly everyone was racing toward the other end of the field.

Up and down the field they raced for the hour and a half that the game lasted. From time to time, I'd catch a glimpse of Zack's face, focused, earnest, but aglow with excitement and passion. Across the field I'd see him stiffen with agony as the other team scored, but then he would be off once again, deeply participating in this game of scoring points by kicking a small white ball into the net.

At the end of the game, Zack was sad that his team hadn't won—they'd missed by a single goal. But even in his sadness, his face was aglow with joy. For me, the images that stuck in my mind from that day became the very epitome of passion and involvement. And I thanked Zack for reminding me of yet another route to happiness.

But how do we capture the kind of joy with life that Zack knew so well during the soccer game? Let me offer some tips on what no one ever told you about how to get happy. They are easy to remember: Just think of a pea pod.

Pretend you have a pea pod in your hand. You open it by gently pulling a string on the bottom of the pod, and there you see three small peas in your pod. You say to yourself, "Wow, I have three P's in my pod." Your P's are Passion, People, and Participation.

Passion. Happiness is fueled by the kind of passion Zack has for soccer. I'm sure his dreams are filled with perfect plays and impossible goals. But how do we find that kind of passion in our own lives? At this moment, you may not be even able to imagine what that would feel like. But have faith! You may find your passion in fleeting moments. Pay attention to those times when you're so deeply engaged in some activity that you lose all sense of time. The chances are very good that this activity can be expanded into your passion. Here's an example from my own life:

I have a passion for gardening. I love my flowers. As I water my rose bushes, I talk to each and every one of them. I caress each petal not only with my fingers but also with my eyes. I appreciate each rose for its color, size, and scent. The red roses come in different intensities of color ranging from a deep burgundy, like a glass of red Merlot wine, to a bright scarlet, or crimson color. When I smell my roses, I feel as though I am deeply inhaling true beauty, bringing me peace and happiness.

When I'm with my flowers, I'm focused solely on them. I'm involved with them, and I lose track of time. I check to see if they're thirsty. Do they need trimming, or are there any insects feasting on them? I'm absorbed in the moment in my garden. I am at one with my surroundings.

Sometimes when my husband and I are going out, before we get into the car, if I see that one of my plants is drooping, I stop everything and water it. My flowers are my friends, and I want to take good care of them. Like friends, it brings me much pleasure to watch them grow and change. My enjoyment lasts as I cut fresh flowers and bring them into my house. It makes me happy to see the flowers every day. This is my passion, and it fills me with a deep sense of satisfaction.

People feel passionate about different things, such as hobbies, volunteer work, or collecting things. I have a friend who collects ceramic frogs. On her travels she buys frogs as souvenirs. Now, I have to confess that frogs aren't my thing. But she says she loves to look at her frogs. When she does, she recalls where each one was purchased and relives the particular place.

Spend some time each day for the next two weeks thinking about what you're really interested in. Ask yourself what you're excited about. What energizes you and makes you feel enthusiastic? Do you do things you consider just hobbies? Maybe these hobbies can be turned into passions. Think about your most enjoyable times. It doesn't matter what you were doing. It only matters that you have an interest. What made these times great for you? It's never too late to develop passion.

If you want to learn about passion, watch children, especially while they play. Observe their behavior. They're fully absorbed in what they're doing each moment. They have vivid imaginations. Just watch a child play with an imaginary friend or jump rope. They stay busy and involved in each activity they're participating in. Children also seem to be very comfortable in nature. I remember when I was about ten years old, my sister Linda and I heard that rainwater was good for your hair. We used to stand outside in heavy downpours of rain rubbing our heads with shampoo, bubbles dripping in our eyes. We grew up in Florida where rain was plentiful, so we had ample opportunity to wash our hair in it. We also collected tiny little black tadpoles in the many puddles that were left standing for days after a heavy rain. We collected them in jars and kept them for weeks until they matured into frogs.

When you listen to a child tell you a story about what they're interested in, you can see and hear the enthusiasm. Their voice is high pitched and eager as they talk fast, with excitement lighting up their face.

For inspiration, and to remember my excitement as a child, I keep in my office a photograph of me as a baby, sitting on the beach near the water, laughing, squealing with joy. Search for such a reminder from your life.

Here are some more hints to help you find your passion. Think of the things you liked to do as a child. Did you win any prizes or receive any special acknowledgments? When I was twelve, I got a medal for swimming shore to shore across a large cold lake. I was the youngest camper to accomplish this feat.

What captivated your imagination in your childhood? What did you pretend? Did you make up games?

Dreams are where it all begins. Remember, happiness is a journey, not a destination. Passion is what gives energy to every step of that journey.

Participation. Our passion is ignited by our participation. We may have a dream of having a rose garden, but until the dream comes alive, we're not truly happy. Dreams become real through our action—and that is participation. That dream can be the seed for our passion. But our passion is not truly ignited until we participate, that is, until we actually get out there and start digging in the dirt.

My aunt Ruth is eighty-five years old. She's young at heart, inspirational, and has an unparalleled zest for life. Her passion is her fashionable dress boutique, which bears her name. She started this business fifty years ago. She has had her share of health troubles and suffered losses in her life, yet she's one of the most engaging people to be around. She is the perfect model for the person who fully participates in life, has passion for what she does, and surrounds herself with positive people. Her favorite expression is, "I'm dancing as fast as I can."

I know of several reasons for Aunt Ruth's success. She is the essence of what it means to participate. She doesn't just dream about things she'd love to do. She dives in and does them and rarely lets her own doubts stop her. That kind of participation takes courage, but simply being in her presence is proof that it all comes back to her as happiness.

Where does your participation start? First catch hold of one of those dreams you've had—about gardening, soccer, volunteering—whatever it is, dive in. Take a class to find out more about it, if you wish. That's the first step in becoming a participator. Read books or find videotapes about the things that interest you. Pretty soon you'll feel your passion rising and you'll know your way.

And now that you have a nice little glow of passion started with the aid of your full participation, it's time to turn that glow into a bonfire. How do you do that? You seek the company of others who share your passion. If you're an avid gardener, maybe you do this by joining a garden club or by opening up conversations with people at the nurseries you frequent. Or maybe your partner, a neighbor, or even a distant friend living on the other side of the country can share your passion. You involve people in your life.

People. Perhaps you're wondering what can people do specifically to help you develop your passion and to participate more fully in life. Seek people connections that can help you maintain your enthusiasm for your passion. Once you've tapped into your passion, you want to share that passion with people who can be equally excited about it with you.

Pretend you're engaged in a conversation with a friend. You're discussing an activity you're passionate about. Your friend is hanging on your every word, listening intently. Their eyes are focused on you. They lean toward you, careful not to miss a word. Your energy and excitement build. Their interest and excitement make you even more excited. Now that's passion!

Contrast this with another person you're speaking to. You try to share your passion with them, but they're barely listening. They don't seem to care what you're saying. You lose your focus; your energy and zest dive-bomb into the pits. Their lack of interest dulls your excitement. The main point here is that associating with people who can share your interests will "amp up" your passion. It allows you to share your excitement and get confirmation that what you're doing is worthwhile. If your passion is roses, share that activity with people of similar mind. Share your passion(s) with people who are equally excited about it. Anything less is just a drain of your happiness. You might want to expand your base of friends who give back as much as you give.

Moving forward. Keep your P's in your pod. Explore your passions and fuel them by taking action and fully participating in the things that interest you. As your participation and passion build, share your excitement with people with similar interests. Their excitement will help expand the passion you feel. These are keys to happiness!

Whistle While
You Work

*Choose a job you love, and you will never have
to work a day in your life.*

–Confucius

Work, work, work! When you wake up on Monday mornings,
are you already longing for Friday? Do you think to yourself, "If
my boss doesn't give me that raise soon, I'm going to leave"?
Then, on your way to work, do you wish you could just keep
going and play hooky? Or are you so wild about your work that
you wake up energized and ready to meet any challenge?

When you've chosen a line of work that's enjoyable, interesting,
and captures your imagination, you're naturally more enthusiastic about it. When your work is meaningful to you, it reflects
that to the world. Try to engage yourself in conversation with
people about their work sometime; it's easy to tell how they
feel. Their eyes either light up and sparkle when speaking or
they generally get a glazed-over look and have little excitement
in their voice.

When you like what you do, it can act as a vaccine against some of nature's ills. People who are happy with their work generally are healthier, both mentally and physically. They have more zest and joy in their life.

A simple change in attitude can make all the difference. If you're not satisfied in your job but feel that a change would be difficult or impossible at this time, a change of attitude can often do wonders. Maybe you're bored. Possibly you need a fresher outlook. Look at your work with new eyes, the ones that see the positive side of your work.

Learn new aspects of your work. Teach yourself better computer skills.

Take an interest in your coworkers. Ask them about themselves and their outside interests.

Look for what's good about your job. Perhaps you have the freedom to choose your own work schedule, or you get benefits such as health insurance, sick leave, and child care.

Start to notice details about your workplace that perhaps you never saw before. Maybe you have a great view (or, if you don't have a window, put up a nature poster so you'll have a better view!).

> Take pride in your accomplishments both big and small. Be thankful that you met your deadlines all week long or closed the deal you've been working on for over a year.

Is it time to move on? Perhaps you're in a job you really hate and have taken enough Pepto-Bismol to paint your house pink. If this is the case, my best advice to you is to quit and start something new. This may sound drastic, but there are ways to start a new career while you're in your present one. For example, you can take night classes in a new field of interest or use weekends to learn a new skill.

There are many resources to help you with a career change. One of the best books on the subject is *What Color Is Your Parachute? A Practical Manual for Job-Hunters and Career-Changers* by Richard Nelson Bolles. There are career counselors, lectures you can attend, and support groups. Many people are finding new job opportunities on the Internet.

Changing careers can be scary, partly because you're changing the known for the unknown. But when you think about the fact that you spend about a quarter of your life on the job and commuting between work and home, don't you want to like what you do for a living? When what you do is fulfilling, you unknowingly whistle while you work; you're composing your own happy tune. If you're not as happy as you want to be in your work but don't like change, ask yourself, **"Am I going to let fear stop me from making a change?"**

One way I teach students to handle fear is to imagine putting their fear into a container. Some think of placing it in a small envelope. Others imagine a steamer trunk so large it won't fit through the door. For example, one of my students who wanted to change careers had an important job interview he was anxious about. He imagined putting his fear into a briefcase, which he toted along with him. By doing this, he overcame his fear because he acknowledged it and wasn't preoccupied with it. It gave him something to do with it.

Where some people say, "Don't give in to your fears," I say, "Take your fear with you and do it anyhow." In this way, you make fear your friend because you're not fighting it.

If you're not whistling while you work, take a few minutes and do the following exercise. Pretend that money is no object and that you have all the educational requirements needed to do whatever work you want. What do you see yourself doing? To help you get in touch with your feelings, ask yourself the following questions:

What are my particular inclinations? Do I want to start my own business or do I prefer working for other businesses?

Whose work do I most admire and what type of work is that?

What are my personal strengths and talents?

You do have the power to choose work that you love. And only you can take control of your life and do it. Don't just dream—make a plan, take action, and make it happen one small step at a time.

18

Use Nature as a Guide to Lead a Happier Life

Happiness is a butterfly, which, when pursued, is always just beyond your grasp, but which, if you will sit down quietly, may alight upon you.

–Nathaniel Hawthorne

Accept the laws of Mother Nature, for they are fundamental to our existence. Think of your mind as the waves of an ocean. The tide rolls in and out. The same is true of our thoughts: they roll in and out of our minds. We don't judge the ocean, or even question the tides.

Think of your environment as a source of strength and connection. Don't take the beauty that surrounds you for granted. Nature can teach you about change because it's always changing.

By experiencing nature, you have the perfect opportunity to bring more peace and joy into your life. Even if you live in a big city, there are parks to walk in, sunrises and sunsets to watch, flowers to smell, and an occasional tree to admire.

Many people tell me they find happiness and a special connection with themselves by being in nature. I have a friend who feels totally at peace when she sits under the redwood trees in Muir Woods in Northern California. This is the place where she is quiet and feels an interconnectedness with the universe.

Other people report feeling peaceful when they're near water. Personally, I love the ocean. I always do a visualization when I'm at the beach watching the waves. I mentally throw whatever challenges I'm dealing with at the moment into the water. I never call them problems. Challenges seem easier to deal with than problems. I watch them wash away from me out to sea. Sometimes I'll pick up small stones and use them symbolically for any challenges I'm having, and when I toss the stones into the water, I say I'm tossing my challenges away. It's a way of letting go. Try it. It'll work for you, too. It's also fun.

Perhaps you feel good in the mountains. I live near the mountains, and whenever I look at them, I feel renewed with a sense of power. My mother used to say, "You can gain great strength from the mountains." She was right.

Nature teaches us many lessons about happiness. If you want more serenity and joy in your life, use nature as your guide. You can start by doing three simple things:

1. LISTEN. Learn to listen. Wherever you are now, take a

moment and close your eyes, be still, and just listen. What do you hear? The birds, the rush of water, the leaves speaking, and the flowers singing as the wind rolls over them. You may hear wildlife. Listen to the insects talking to each other in a language foreign to you. Animals make sounds that only they can understand. Listening to the sounds of nature, you begin to learn about yourself because you're part of nature.

2. **LOOK.** Become an avid observer. Look at everything as though you're seeing it for the first time. Go ahead, pretend you're a child and pick up a stone. You'll see colors that perhaps you never noticed before. Take some water and wet the stone. Look at the difference. Imagine you're a landscape artist. Take your imaginary paints and brushes and paint your mental masterpiece as only you see it.

Look at the many shades of blue in the sky. Notice all the variations of green in the foliage. There are more hues in the outdoors than you can count, because colors change with the light. By observing nature, we see that it's always changing. The colors and the landscape change, depending on the seasons. Likewise, we're forever changing, depending on our emotional and physical well-being. Allow yourself to change at your own pace.

3. **LINGER.** The seasons linger. The leaves fall slowly from the trees. The branches become bare. The sky gradually turns gray and the

first snow starts to fall. Then the ground begins to thaw and small buds appear. The spring bloom begins, and nature seems more alive. Summer seems to linger forever, but then it slowly begins to change and the leaves begin to fall.

Nature is not in a hurry to change. Yet if we don't change our personalities, appearances, and behavior all at once, we're disappointed. Learn from nature. Learn to linger.

Finding your place in nature can have a calming effect and renew your spirit. You can meditate and relax in YOUR SPECIAL SPOT. Find that place in nature—the garden, forest, mountains, water, or wherever nature takes you where you feel peaceful—and quiet your mind. Remember to visit that place often.

Observe Happy People and Imitate Their Behavior

The happiest people are those who think the most interesting thoughts. Those who decide to use leisure as a means of mental development, who love good music, good books, good pictures, good company, good conversation, are the happiest people in the world.

–William Lyon Phelps

What do happy people have in common? Pretend for a moment you're at a party where there are twenty-four guests. You're merely an observer, a fly on the wall. Twelve of the guests are happy and twelve are unhappy. It's up to you to spot the differences between the two groups and discover the similar traits of the happy guests. What might you notice first? Are the happy people laughing and the unhappy people scowling? Are the happy people carefree and the unhappy people glum? You probably notice that all the happy people are enthralled with the conversations they're involved in, while the unhappy people seem anxious and distracted.

It's relatively easy to spot the more apparent traits of happy people, like the ones mentioned above. However, there are other traits that aren't so visible. After talking to many people about the traits of happy people, I've reached the conclusion that happy people tend to

* **Be filled with hope.** *When you have hope, you don't give up. Along with hope comes the feeling of optimism. Being optimistic is training yourself to think everything will be okay. When faced with a challenge in your life, it's important to hang on to hope. For example, people who have been lost at sea or in the mountains say they never gave up hope of being found.*

* **Have faith.** *One often hears people who have experienced a tragedy say, "It was my faith that got me through." This faith makes you believe that you can handle whatever life hands you and you'll survive.*

* **Accept themselves.** *Happy people tend to accept themselves as they are. They know they're not perfect. They don't constantly judge themselves, nor do they criticize themselves for what they can't do. They concentrate on their strengths, not their weaknesses.*

* **Possess high self-esteem.** *When you have good self-esteem—a general feeling that you're a capable, lovable, and worthwhile person—you develop self-confidence. Therefore, you feel good about yourself. If you feel good about yourself, there's no need*

to put someone else down.

Help others. Happy people tend to go out of their way to help other people. They undertake volunteer work in their communities. They tend to be socially adept, and they establish long-lasting friendships as well as easily create new friendships. People who call themselves advocates truly enjoy giving to others. They derive a lot of personal satisfaction from it and it brings them happiness.

Keep busy. There's a saying, "If you want to get something done, give it to a busy person." Happy people keep busy with interesting things. If you're active, you accomplish more because you're more efficient with your time. There's a fine line between the person who is **too** busy and a person who has a busy, interesting life. Keep yourself busy enough to enjoy life, but not so busy that your loved ones feel they need to make an appointment with you.

Have control over their lives. People who realize they have choices in life feel empowered. If you believe you have the power to control your destiny, then you'll feel more in control of your life. Happy people also know there are certain things in life they can't control, such as losses of all kinds. Therefore, to be happy you need to be realistic about those things you can and cannot control.

Enjoy having fun. Happy people know they can work hard and play hard. They take time to play. They're not afraid to be silly and have fun. Give yourself permission to go out and have a good time. "A good time comes in handy," as my mother used to say.

Not take themselves too seriously. If you don't take yourself too seriously, you can laugh at yourself and some of the absurdities of life. Laughter gives us a new perspective on life. Personally, I keep a quote by Gail Parent over my desk that reads, "She knew what all smart women knew: Laughter made you live better and longer."

Forgive themselves and others. One of the best gifts you can give yourself is to forgive and recognize that you're human and fallible. Hopefully, you can learn from your mistakes. People who are able to give themselves the treasure of forgiving themselves and others almost always receive the by-product of happiness. This is because when you forgive, you open the door to freeing yourself of the past.

Care about their appearance. Happy people know that if they look good, they feel better, because they have more confidence and feel better about themselves.

I'm sure everyone will recognize a few of these traits in themselves. To become happier, observe happy people. You might discover a few more traits you'd like to have. Look for them, imitate them, and you'll gradually make your journey happier in the process.

Love Yourself
and Others

*You will find as you look back upon your life that the moments
when you have really lived are the moments when you have
done things in the spirit of love.*

–Henry Drummond

What's love got to do with happiness? Everything! Your life's
journey is happier when it's filled with love. Loving yourself is
the most meaningful of all love. If you don't love yourself, you
can't love anyone else. **There is no one more important than
you are.**

As a young child, our family spent a lot of time with my Uncle
Billy. We would go over to his house for dinner and the table
would be set with the best china, the finest silver, and the fresh-
est flowers. I would always ask, "Uncle Billy, who else is coming to dinner? Are you having company?" He would reply, "No,
it's just us." It was puzzling to me that all this finery was set out
for just us, the family. So I'd ask why. To this day, I remember
his reply: "There's no one who is better company than we are,
Will. It's important to always treat yourself as a guest." This is

a philosophy I've lived by ever since. When you think of yourself as a guest, you're treating yourself with love.

Some people may have gotten the message when they were young that self-love was selfish and narcissistic. Nothing could be further from the truth. In fact, it's essential that you develop self-love. When you love yourself, you realize that it's easy to

Stop criticizing yourself.

Develop compassion and kindness toward yourself.

*Proceed on your own journey. Your journey may be different from other people's, or different from what other people think **yours** should be.*

By doing these things, you become self-accepting but at the same time more accepting of others. You acquire compassion for others. You criticize others less. You have more friends. You realize other people cannot MAKE YOU HAPPY OR UNHAPPY. Only you can do this for yourself.

Love is essential to happiness. Most people agree that a key element to their happiness is love. They fantasize about love. They put great expectations on it. They think if only they had a tremendous amount of love in their lives they would be happy. Well, if you don't love yourself before you fall in love with someone else, your happiness will be short lived.

Love is not a panacea to all of life's pains. While it's true that the more love you have in your life the better you'll feel, it's not a cure-all for everything. Love doesn't conquer all if you don't love yourself.

Become an LOL—a lover of life! Appreciate everything and take nothing for granted.

The true and false about love and happiness. An easy way to remind yourself of what is true and false about love and happiness, while keeping a sense of humor, is to think about the following:

L—is for the way he/she looks at me.

People who fall in love at first sight are usually shortsighted. They say wistfully, "I saw him/her across a crowded room, our eyes met, and it was love."

Looks are fine. Wishful thinking is okay, too. Just keep your eyes open and live in the real world. One of the difficulties of doing that may be that reality seems boring. You prefer action, excitement, lust, and instant gratification from your love relationships all at the same time. Needless to say, romantic love can have its dangers.

O—is being open to LOVE.

Be willing to take a chance on love, even if you've been hurt in the past. Look within to see that you're a worthwhile, lovable person just the way you are.

V—is for vulnerability.

Love can make you feel vulnerable. When you love or are in love in a safe environment, you're willing to risk being vulnerable. Otherwise, if you don't feel safe, you may feel helpless or powerless. A friend once commented to me about her fiancé, "Now he knows all my secrets. What if he uses them against me?" This woman didn't feel secure in her relationship.

E—is for everyone.

Love is for everyone. Everyone deserves love.

There are many ways to increase love in your life.

Act in a loving way.

Don't look for fault with yourself or others.

Be caring and loving toward yourself and others.

Love has the ability to transform an ordinary occasion into a joyous one. Let love embrace you and all those around you and bring you happiness in return. **What's love got to do with happiness??? Everything!!!**

21

Lend a Helping Hand to Others

The road to daily happiness is not hard to find. It's what we do for others that brings us peace of mind.

–Unknown

Don't wait for a need, do a good deed. Giving of yourself, which can include your time, talents, energy, or money, has its own reward in bringing you happiness. This is especially true if you give of yourself freely, without expectation of return or reward. Happiness CAN follow. I call this "giving of the heart." You give from your heart because you're a kind, benevolent person.

Bruce Williams, an attorney and photographer, illustrates this point:

In order to be happy, one must literally share his heart. He must share his life and embrace his fellow man so that he is vulnerable and humble among his fellow man. Acts of kindness and selflessness must be achieved constantly and consistently—and absolutely without the expectation of personal gain of any kind.

In these objectives all of us fail to a degree, but unless we achieve serenity and altruism, we will *not* be happy. Unless we know within ourselves that we have shown kindness and nurtured the welfare of others, we will not be happy. When we do these things, we can smile from the inside out—and that is the only true smile, and that is the only true happiness.

The art of giving rewards you with positive feelings about yourself. When you're giving, you don't have time to think about yourself or to fixate on what's wrong with you. You can forget about your own troubles for the moment. Often, when you do this, you get a better perspective on the challenges you face in life. Take the focus off yourself and turn it to others. You can do this by giving

* *Compliments*
* *Appreciation*
* *Service to others*
* *Encouragement*
* *Smiles*

Volunteer work presents a great opportunity to feel good about yourself and experience different areas of interest. There are many ways to volunteer in your community. Numerous organizations need your help. Giving of your time can also help you meet new people. And there's always room in our lives for more interesting people.

My friend Marlene is a widow who lives by herself and never had children. She has no immediate family. Yet, she's one of the happiest people I know. She is the purest example of giving. Marlene is an excellent cook. She prepares meals with love, and friends eagerly look forward to an invitation to her dinner parties. She has friends of all ages. She is an interesting person who doesn't wait for life to happen. She creates it by extending herself to others, expecting nothing in return. **When you bring light into someone else's life, you illuminate your own.**

How do you rate on the giving scale? People need you and your special talents. For instance, you can read a story to a lonely old man in a nursing home. Think about how fortunate you are that just by doing such a small thing, you were able to bring some happiness into another person's life. When you give of yourself and your time without thinking of getting something back, the rewards come back to you, and the good feeling you have about yourself doubles your joy.

22

Don't Take Yourself TOO Seriously

Of all days, the day on which one has not laughed is surely the most wasted.

–S. Chamfort

Lighten up! I always carry a feather in my bag. It serves as a reminder to take myself lightly. Feathers also tickle. When I find myself being too serious, I use the feather to tickle myself and it makes me laugh. Sometimes I hand out feathers after one of my seminars because I want the participants to remember to take themselves lightly, too.

It's extremely important to develop a lightheartedness about life if you want to be happy. It's something children seem to exhibit as a natural extension of their temperaments. As a child, you had it, too, but you lost it. You were told to "Grow up," "Stop laughing," "Don't be silly." But now it's time to get your lightheartedness back. It'll help get you through some tough times.

Take your average day, for instance. There can be a lot of annoyances—some days more than others. It's easy to become irritated and upset. During these times your lightheartedness is tested. Before you scream and pull your hair out, take a look at the big picture. Are you still breathing air? Can you still put one foot in front of the other, even though it may feel like you're climbing Mount Everest? If you can, remind yourself that it's a GOOD day!

Up close and personal. We all need to develop a sense of perspective about things, like painters who step back to view their paintings. It becomes a different painting when seen from a distance. Up close, they may just see a mass of brush strokes that don't look like anything in particular. It's only by standing back that the painter sees the image.

You can do the same with your life. You can gain some perspective. You just need to stand back from the challenges you face in your life and take in the broader picture. Pretend you're someone else looking at your life. When you're able to stand back and observe, sometimes things are not as bad as they seem. You see solutions. You notice options that remained hidden when you were so caught up with yourself. For instance, have you ever noticed how easy it is to give advice to friends about their lives? That's because you can stand back and get a better perspective than they have. It's harder to fix your own life because you're so close to it and you lose your objectivity.

Uptight? Everything is all right. Almost everyone has looked back at things they took far too seriously and had a good laugh at them.

Think of the wasted energy you expended when you took things too seriously. What can you do to lighten up? First of all, take a look inside your Happiness Instruction Kit. There's always something there to help you. For starters, here are five tools for alleviating "overseriousness" dilemmas that are not as disastrous as you may think:

1. *Remember that things could always be worse. Never ask, "Oh God, what else could go wrong?"*

2. *Ask yourself, "Will THIS matter ten years from now, five years or even next year?"*

3. *Use humor. Laugh at yourself. Use funny expressions. When someone asks you, "How is your day?" You might reply, "I'm having a salmon day." (This is the kind of day where you feel like you're swimming upstream.)*

4. *Always carry a feather!*

5. *Recall the times you worried about things. STOP BEING A WORRIER AND BECOME A WARRIOR!*

For the past thirty-five years, my friend Phyllis Berkett has had a worry box. She told me, "Personally, I only worry on Wednesdays. But you can choose any day. You'd be surprised how few worries ever become anything monumental when you put them away for a week. I think this plays a large part in making my life a happy one."

Create your own worry box. Find an old shoe box in your closet or a discarded Christmas box in the basement. Any box will do. Don't worry about it! Pick a day, any day, and let that be the day you use your worry box. Take several scraps of paper and write down all your worries—one worry per scrap of paper. Put the scraps in the box and don't think about your worries. Once you've written them down, you've given them over to the worry box. Then, in a week's time, go back to the box and tear up the scraps of paper. If you choose, reread your worries first. You'll be surprised at how many of them have disappeared.

Make sure your happiness kit includes a good sense of humor and some feathers. After all, there's no humor in taking yourself too seriously.

23

Learn to Manage Your Stress Effectively

When one is happy, there is no time to be stressed;
being happy engrosses the whole attention.

–Unknown

Has your life become a stress factory? Are you manufacturing stress? I have a friend who says he always wakes up happy. At the risk of calling him a liar, I asked him if he has a special secret. He smiled and said, "No, not really. I just listen to happy music in the morning and think only about all the good things I'll be doing during the day." To my friend, happy music is anything that doesn't startle him awake, something that's fun and upbeat but not too loud. After a peaceful night's sleep, he prefers not to have a rock band blast him out of bed at the break of dawn. But then rock music might work for you.

My friend has taught me other things, too, about starting the day stress free. He gives himself extra time in the morning so he doesn't feel rushed. I've found this to be excellent advice, since I used to time things to the wire if I had to be someplace.

I used to literally run for planes, so that by the time I got to the terminal, I looked like I had just run a marathon.

The point is, the extra five minutes you allow yourself in the morning can set the tone of your whole day—one that's relaxing and less prone to anxiety.

Doing your best, but your life is still full of stress? For many people, it seems their entire life has become just that—a basketful of stress. Undoubtedly, there has always been stress in people's lives, but they didn't talk about it. Perhaps there was a different kind of stress in past generations, one of merely trying to survive rather than dealing with the anxieties of current living, such as our busy schedules, a polluted environment, and the violence around us.

Whatever the source of your stress, you're not alone—everyone experiences it in their daily lives, some more than others. Assuredly, being stressed can add up to different things for different people. For some people, real stress is as simple as their bananas ripening and rotting before they get a chance to eat them, or when they can't find their remote control for the TV. For others, being stressed is when they're dealing with a life-threatening illness or loss of a job. One type of stress you can do something about, the other you can't. How do you define your stress?

Can't say no? This is one cause of undue stress. If you're the type of person who gets locked into obligations you don't particularly want, then perhaps you need to find a way to say "no." There are three answers you can give:

🌸 *"I can't say 'yes' to that right now."*

🌸 *"I think I'll pass on that one."*

🌸 *"No, but thank you for asking."*

Write these down on a 3" x 5" card and keep them as cue cards by your telephone at home and on your desk at work.

Other reasons for undue stress include sleep deprivation, dealing with toxic people, and worrying about future disasters that will probably never happen.

Stress is a popular topic. There are stress management classes all over the country. Pick up any health magazine and you can find dozens of antistress formulas to counter life's negative influences. There are aromatherapy stress-relieving recipes for the bath. There are antistress vitamins. There are products for our overstressed hair! Even our skin is stressed! The media inundates us with images of relaxed, destressed models in order to sell more products and get us into expensive spas. The media also saturates us with stressful news reports, docudramas, and movies that often cause us to experience a free-floating anxiety that adds up to more stress in our lives.

What can you do about stress? First ask yourself, "Where is my stress coming from? Is it real or imagined stress?" Imagined stress is something you think *might* happen. It hasn't happened yet, but you're anxious about it. Imagined stress is thinking the worst will happen in a situation. For example, you're sure you'll fail your upcoming driver's test. You're so anxious about taking the test that you can't sleep at night. You dream about parallel parking. What's important to keep in mind is that this test you're overly stressed or worried about has not yet happened. It's the anticipation that's causing you stress. Wouldn't it be more constructive to imagine you'll do well on the test?

When you feel stressed out, ask yourself three questions:

1. *Is there anything I can do about the stress in this situation? Do I have control?*

2. *Is there a way I can calm myself so that I can think clearly?*

3. *How best do I take care of myself in this stressful situation?*

Here are some more simple stress busters. Rummage through your happiness kit and you'll find just what you need to remove some of the stress in your life. To begin with, try out the following six stress busters:

1. *Breathe deeply. We forget to breathe, not entirely, of course,*

but deeply.

2. *Write down your stresses on a piece of paper and tear the paper to shreds.*

3. *Visualize yourself surrounded by white light for protection against the stress.*

4. *Laugh. You don't need a reason.*

5. *Take a five-minute break during the day. Call it your "me-me" break.*

6. *Get a toy boat or even a popsicle stick. Fill up your bathtub or sink with water and think of your stress as being on that toy boat or stick. Imagine it diminishing as it floats in the water. Take the drain plug out, remove your boat or stick, and watch the water drain. Visualize your stress going down the drain with it.*

On your journey to happiness, don't permit stress to paralyze you. When you're feeling stressed and you're worrying about everything, you often accomplish nothing. You become overwhelmed and confused to the point of becoming immobilized. Now is the time to prioritize and learn to do only one thing at a time. You can accomplish more when your stress level is lower and you are relaxed.

Laugh Your Way
to Happiness

After God created the world, He made man and woman.
Then, to keep the whole thing from collapsing, He invented humor.

–Mack McGinnis

Become a laughaholic. When Beaumont was fifteen years old, he told me that he wanted to contribute to this book, I asked him what he wanted to write about. He said "laughter," because as a family we laugh a lot. I was delighted in his interest and curious what he would come up with about laughter. Here it is:

I've always thought that there are four kinds of people in the world: those who laugh, those who don't, those who make us laugh, and those who wonder how the people who make us laugh do so. I feel sorry for those people who can't laugh and for those who wonder how people make others laugh. I suppose the reason I feel sorry for those people is because they don't know what they're missing. Laughter really is the best medicine. It can make you feel better even in the darkest moments. When I think of some of the hardest times in my life, I end up in tears from laughing almost every time.

I find happiness in laughter. My mother is a laughaholic (a person who laughs uncontrollably). I suppose some of it has rubbed off onto me. She laughs at the strangest things. We'll be in the middle of an argument and she'll break out laughing. At first I'm bewildered, but then I end up laughing, too. I guess that's why I love her so much.

Humor is high octane. Ten minutes of laughter releases your endorphins and helps your cardiovascular system. Norman Cousins, former editor of *Saturday Review* and a proponent of healing by laughter, called laughter "inner jogging." He believed that "when we are engaged in a good hearty laugh, every system in our body gets a workout."

The more humor you find in situations, the more you can see the absurdities of life and the more everyday fun you'll experience. I've learned that the most embarrassing moments are the ones I laugh most about later. I think this is why TV blooper shows are so popular. Actors and actresses are famous for making bloopers. That's why it sometimes takes thirty tries to get one good take.

Happiness and humor go together. You can't have one without the other. They enhance each other. Happier people are humorous and humorous people are often happier. They're hard to separate.

One of the easiest ways to become happier is to see the humor in your daily life. It's eternally present. Who hasn't developed a major case of the DROPsies or SPILLitis at least once in their lifetime? You just have to look for the comedy in your life, become attuned to it, and develop a knack for recognizing it. When you acquire these skills, it'll help you lighten up. Always remember, today's trauma will be tomorrow's drama.

Humor is a good tool for survival. Having a sense of humor promotes better mental and physical health. Life can be difficult. It's not always about sweetness and light or fun and games. It's also about losses and misfortunes. Humor can be used as a coping mechanism, one that's often overlooked. This brings to mind my grandfather's funeral. You might ask, How funny could that be? As a rule, I don't find funerals funny, but the following incident is one I'll never forget.

On the way to the cemetery after my grandfather's funeral, the hearse carrying his body got a flat tire. The driver pulled over and announced a slight delay. We had all been crying until we suddenly remembered that "Poppy" was always having some sort of car trouble in his lifetime. Even on the day of his funeral, it continued. Our tears of sorrow immediately turned to hardy laughter. So, you see, when you use humor to cope, it helps you deal with your pain and suffering. Use humor to your advantage.

Humor eases your pain by distracting you from your discomfort. It gives you time to refocus and releases the tension and stress that loss and pain cause. In periods of hardship, time is what is often important. That's why we say, "Time heals all wounds." Laughter can give you that little extra time to distract your mind, so if the pain comes again, perhaps you'll look at it in a different way.

The traumas you go through can even become comical after some time has passed. Remembering this can greatly ease your emotional turmoil. For example, people *love* to talk about their operations. They even like to show you their scars. They can laugh about being left on the gurney, or writing in ink on their leg, "Do not operate on this leg. It's the other leg." But at the time of the operation, things weren't so funny. Time creates a new perspective that makes room for laughter later on. As Charlie Chaplin said, "Life is a tragedy when seen in closeup but a comedy in long shot."

Let's explore three tools in your happiness kit to help keep humor in your life. I use these a lot, and if you use them, I know they'll show you other ways you can add daily laughter to everyday life. This may take some practice. After all, being a stand-up comic isn't easy!

Exaggerate. This is an easy way to make uncomfortable moments something to laugh about. For example, if you're having a bad day, look at the clock and take exactly fifteen minutes to complain about all that's gone wrong. Be as dramatic as possible. Pretend you're auditioning for the Soap Opera Awards. Use hand and body gestures as much as possible to enhance your performance. Complain out loud about everything that's awful in your life at the moment (e.g., "Nobody loves me," "My relationship is in the pits," "I hate my job"). You may run out of steam before your fifteen minutes are up. You'll probably become bored with yourself and even laugh.

Exaggeration can take many forms. Writing an exaggerated letter can help you deal with a catastrophe. I have a client who once wrote a letter to his deceased father, who didn't include my client in his will. It went something like this:

Dear Disowned Dad,

Thanks for NOTHING$$$. Where's my trust account you promised me OVER AND OVER AGAIN? Do you think for one minute I would have visited you so often in the retirement home if I'd known you were only dangling the trust fund in front of me like a carrot and had no intention of ever giving me a dime? Instead, you left the money to some woman I never heard of. She's probably on a world cruise with her claws into some other millionaire *who's about to croak. I guess you thought she needed the money more than your own son.*

Your ungrateful, greedy son,

George, Jr.

When you practice exaggerating your anger, hurts, and troubles as George did, you begin to gain some perspective and see how ludicrous your circumstances are. It's then that you begin to forgive and let laughter dissolve the problem.

Use reinforcements. This has to do with the psychology of props. Employ items that help take the edge off a situation and save your sanity.

WARNING—Don't try these unless you can live with the idea that you might look like an idiot or a complete fool. Go for it. Dare to be outrageous. I carry certain props with me all the time. They include:

Big red wax lips—perfect for traffic, anywhere. Don't carry them around in the summertime. (They'll melt.) They're very popular around Halloween.

A laughing ball—A laughing ball is small and fits in your hand. All you have to do is turn it on, carry it in your pocket, and it laughs a lot. This is good for any tense situation. Be prepared to get odd looks from strangers on this one, since people don't know where the laughing is coming from.

* **A happy face button**—*This always brings a smile to people's faces.*

* **Bubbles**—*Blowing bubbles is joyous. Just look at a child's face when you blow bubbles in the air. Think about putting your anxieties in a bubble and blowing them away.*

Find some props of your own that can ease your anxieties and tension and lower your stress level. Use them daily.

Do the unexpected. People are creatures of habit. We do the same things day after day. We get up at the same time, have the same thing for breakfast and lunch. We drive to work and back home, taking the same route. We have dinner at the same time. We talk to the same people. No wonder we feel tired and bored every so often. It's time to liven up our lives. Start today. Here are some simple things you can do to lighten up and surprise yourself and others by doing something out of the ordinary:

* *If your partner or spouse is upset with you, start speaking in a foreign language or start talking gibberish. You've nothing to lose, since he or she is already angry with you. It just might help to lighten up the situation.*

* *If you're feeling bored or out of sorts, take in two double features. Buy some popcorn and, yes, you do want butter!*

Be a tourist for a day—in your own town. Visit the zoo, a museum, or some other local attraction you've never explored. Take your camera and have others take YOUR picture along the way!

Put a note on your office door. Instead of "Out to Lunch," write "Gone Fishing," and take an extra half hour for lunch. This could be risky if you're not the boss!

Camp in or camp out. Set up a tent in your living room or in your own backyard and spend the night. Why not? Kids do it. Just be prepared for some silliness.

Never give up on humor. Keep your life full of fun and frolic. A woman I met while traveling summed it all up when she said, "If you don't have a sense of humor, life will eat you up alive." Another woman I met said, "A hearty laugh is like an instant vacation."

Humor is something you always carry with you in your happiness kit. When you develop a sense of humor, you like and appreciate yourself more. It gives you better ways of coping with life on a daily basis. So, put on your happy helmet and giggle goggles (they're in the kit, too!) and see the world in a humorous way. It's fun. Make your life's journey a playful one.

25

Give YOURSELF a Happiness Lift

Happiness is a habit to be cultivated.

-Unknown

Have you prepared more for your death than for your life? There are many people who get more caught up in preparing for death and the afterlife than paying attention to what they do while they're still visitors here. Are you one of those people? If so, maybe it's time for you to become more mindful of what you can do right now to bring more joy into your life.

Humans constantly plan for their futures. We hire lawyers to draw up prenuptial agreements and living wills. We leave directions for what to do with our material belongings and property when we pass away. We appoint attorneys-in-fact and executors of our estate, prepurchase cemetery plots, and make our wishes known about possible organ transplants. Estate planning and preparing for the next world is big and important business. But what about NOW? Are you living in the present and making happiness a priority?

Develop happy habits. People often ask me, "What can I do NOW to make myself happy? Should I be doing something that I'm not doing? Should I not do something that I am doing?" These are such common questions that I've come up with ten tools to give yourself a happiness lift. I like to think of it as my mini-action happiness plan. If you follow some of these suggestions, they can become a habit. Mark Twain said, "Habit is a habit and not to be flung out of the window by any man but coaxed downstairs a step at a time." All habits come about over time, so you'll need to practice the following as often as possible:

Gratitude promotes a better attitude! Be gracious and be thankful for the good things you hold in your life. Remember the gratitude journal. Write down what you're grateful for as well as what you like about yourself.

Fake it and you will make it. Act happy, even if you're not ecstatic about life at the moment. It's more likely things will improve if you pretend that you feel great and that your life is working just the way you want it to.

Rock and roll is good for the soul. Develop a collection of music that makes you feel good. Listening to music can change your mood immediately. Sing along.

Enhance with dance. You don't need to join the Arthur Murray

Dance Studio to jitterbug around the house. Dance by yourself and let it rip. It will cheer you up and energize you at the same time.

Breathe and relieve. Take a break and breathe deeply. It's the best relaxation tool.

Remedy with comedy. Watch a funny movie. Buy a joke book. Keep your television tuned to the comedy channel. Laughter brings on a happy spirit.

Make out with a workout. You'll always succeed with a bit of happiness when you exercise. Join a gym. Take your abs to the garden, mow the lawn, wash your car, or do some housecleaning. Do what you like, just move your body.

Take a mental health break. This is when you do nothing at all. You haven't assigned yourself anything to do except relax. Even if it's Saturday, forget about the chores.

Stay joyous by being generous. Give to others. Show people that you care. It doesn't take a lot of time to write a note or make a phone call to tell someone you're thinking of them. The best part of this habit is that you fill your heart and another's with joy.

Smile a lot, whether you feel like it or not. If you meet a person without a smile, give them one of yours and see what happens.

Whatever is working in your life, do more of it. It doesn't have to be anything extraordinary. For example, if you start the morning by talking to your plants and it makes you greet the day with a better frame of mind, talk away. I have even given my plants names. This gives both my plants and me a happiness lift.

Keep an open mind to adding new ideas, experiences, and people to your life. Develop an intellectual curiosity. A seventy-five-year-old client of mine attended a lecture where the speaker talked about the composer, Bach, and mentioned that Bach had twenty-two children. My client found this so fascinating that she went out and learned everything she could about the composer.

26

Surround Yourself
with Colors
You Like

You are the artist of your own destiny.

-Unknown

Color yourself happy! Have you ever noticed how children like
to ask each other "What's your favorite color?" Well, personally, I've never heard them reply "Black" or "White." Green, yellow, blue, purple, or orange are often among the color respons-
es kids will give. Just look at the colors they wear—and their
combinations! They're bright, innovative, and snappy! Kids
have pizzazz when it comes to the gear they wear. And most
kids are basically happy.

Many studies have been done on color and how it affects personality and mood. Some colors may cause you to become anxious, while others relax you. When your mind is peaceful, you
may experience a heightened sense of awareness about colors.
As an experiment, try sitting quietly among a field of daisies,
under a tree, or in some other favorite nature spot, and notice

how the colors look brighter and how many different hues there are in the landscape.

Experiment with colors in other ways and see how different ones affect your mood. Become aware of colors that you see every day. For example, the next time you go shopping for apparel, take note of the colors you like. Check out your closet. Do you see all the same colors hanging there? Do you like those colors?

Movie cowboy legend Gene Autry loved the color red. He was the owner of the Angels baseball team, and when it was suggested to him that the uniforms be updated, leaving out the red on the shoes, stirrups, and caps, Autry was disappointed. He told his associates that when he was growing up in Texas, the circus would come to town with its bright red circus wagons. The color red represented fun to Gene Autry, and so it was a color that meant a lot to him. He thought kids should see red in the baseball uniforms because baseball is a fun sport. Although they changed the main colors in the Angels' uniforms, the bill of the home team cap remained red in Autry's honor.

Surround yourself with colors you like in your home, at the office, or even in the color of your car. You probably already know what colors make you feel happy. But in case you're still wondering what all this fanfare is about colors, take a look at what research suggests are the effects that colors have on human beings. You can use it as a guide.

RED—Bold, strong, aggressive, passionate. The red rose is an expression of young love. Millions are sold on Valentine's Day.

GREEN—Healthy, tranquil, soothing. So much of what we see in nature is green.

BLUE—Secure, faithful, authoritative. Blue is the most popular color.

YELLOW—Positive. Most people will greet the day more enthusiastically when they wake up to sunshine.

PURPLE—Royal, expensive. Can create mystery.

BROWN—Earthy, utilitarian, woodsy. Can make you feel grounded.

PINK—Soft, healthy. Gives a sense of sweet peacefulness.

ORANGE—Exuberant, cheerful, fun. Lifts your spirits.

GRAY—Practical, authoritative, somber. Adds stability to your surroundings.

BLACK—Bold, classic, serious. Adds an element of timelessness.

WHITE—Pure, truthful, contemporary. Gives a free-floating feeling.

Mural artist Lori Leahy uses color to enhance her home environment the way she does her murals. She recently told me:

I just painted the ceiling in my bedroom blue, and it affects how I feel in the evening and in the morning when I get up. It's like the sky. It's vast, open, and full of possibilities. When I wake up and look at the ceiling, I feel anything can happen that day.

In my work I use a lot of red. For me, red expresses anger, fear, and rage. It's a very alive color. There's a lot of intensity in the color red. I surround the red with other colors according to the feelings I want to evoke. All colors seem to guide my mood and feelings, as I'm so color sensitive.

Remember, each of the colors you choose to live with can influence your mood and emotions. Pay attention to colors you're attracted to and make mental notes about how they make you feel. If a color makes you feel uncomfortable, it's obviously not for you.

Become your own colorist. Think of everything around you as a giant coloring book. You have crayons in all colors of the spectrum at your disposal. Use them to color yourself happy!

27

Develop Your Spiritual Side, Become a Happy Soul

People who believe in a higher power,
something greater than themselves, seem to be happier.

-David Myers

So much unhappiness comes from the belief that anything good that comes to us has to come from our own efforts. We feel like we have to do the whole thing on our own, that we can't depend on any outside help. I'm convinced that many of us suffer from headaches and backaches because of this. We carry the weight of the world on our shoulders. When we're in the midst of difficult times, we can't see beyond the burdens we're carrying at that moment. We're just certain that if we drop the ball, we'll be crushed under its weight, like in the Roadrunner cartoons where a rock the size of a Greyhound bus falls on Wyle E. Coyote.

We occasionally meet people who are dealing with seemingly impossible challenges yet who go through life with a smile on their face and a song in their heart. You have to wonder what could these people be thinking. Don't they know the sky is falling? Well, the truth is that they do know. But they also know better than to try to hold it up!

There's so much to learn from those who face great challenges with such grace. I have a friend, Betty Hatch, who owned her own modeling agency. She is also a busy community activist. She told me a story illustrating how in her time of struggle she turned to a higher power. She said:

To me, happiness is a feeling of well-being, of calm, of peace of mind. There was a time when life seemed repetitious, tiring, unexciting, filled with endless activity, turmoil, and upsets. Caring for two small boys, running my own business with a huge staff, cooking, and maintaining an active social life, had become more than I could bear. I remember driving down the freeway wondering how I could handle it all. In despair, I said to God, "I give up. You'll have to take over now." And that is exactly what happened. I learned to say no to people and commitments that weren't bringing me peace of mind.

Betty no longer carries the weight of the world on her shoulders, although the truth is that she still has just as many responsibilities and at least as many demands on her life. So where does her peace of mind and her faith come from? How has she developed the kind of trust she has?

I don't want to make it sound too easy. You especially need a big dose of faith when that big boulder comes hurtling down from the sky. There will be times when you feel just like Wyle E. Coyote, flattened like a pancake underneath it. When I become overwhelmed with doubt, I mentally throw my particular challenge up in the sky and ask the universe for help. When my son was born, my life gave new meaning to the term "nervous wreck." The delivery left me in fragile health. I was told I would have permanent high blood pressure. This, along with caring for a newborn and suffering through endless weeks of sleep deprivation, nearly did me in. That's when I made a conscious decision to trust in my higher self. I began daily meditations, and in time my blood pressure decreased. I was able to get off the prescribed medication. The universe had stepped in and allowed each day to get better and better.

Understanding higher sources. What exactly are we saying when we use terms like *higher power* and *higher self*? Like the word *God*, most of us have our own understandings and our own interpretations of these concepts. They imply that there is something—some power either within us, or outside us, or maybe both—that supports us in our lives. There is an underlying belief in what some call the "invisible reality." We all have examples of this reality. For instance, we have felt the invisible bond of the love a mother feels for her children, or that a husband and wife feel for each other. Or we experience a sense of awe when we look up at the sky at night and feel that there is a power far greater than ourselves that is behind it all. These are all invisible in the ordinary sense. But no one would deny their impact on us.

Our experience that there must be a higher power guiding our lives can come in many different ways. Sometimes, plans we had on our own don't work out. Then something better comes along to take its place. For example, a client of mine, Frank, had worked at the same job for fifteen years. He was a photographer working for a magazine. One day his boss called him into the office and announced that the company was downsizing. As much as he hated to do it, he was letting Frank go.

Frank was devastated. He and his wife had two young children, as well as the usual house and medical bills to pay. Getting laid off couldn't have happened at a worse time. Though he had always worked full time for a large company, he had always dreamed of becoming a freelancer. However, he hadn't had the nerve to quit his job or forego a steady paycheck. Now he had time to get his own business started. He and his wife talked it over and decided it was the right time to give it a try. Seemingly out of the blue, an old friend contacted him and hired him to shoot all the products for a new catalog his company was putting together. This job won him other referrals. Within a year, business was booming. Out of what at first seemed a disaster, Frank moved into a position to have his dream come true.

It is stories like these that make us take a closer look at how life really works. Such *turning points* can cause us to wonder if maybe our own plans are never as complete as we think they are. And interestingly enough, when we begin letting go and trusting a higher power, we are often forced to see that we don't have to *do it all ourselves*. The universe, and the higher powers that are apparently in charge of it, will show us the way if only we will not try so hard to impose our own will on it.

One of my clients, Candace, had been raised with religious beliefs. When she was thirty, she experienced the sad death of her beloved brother James, who lost his battle with cancer. After James's death, Candace questioned *why* this brother who she had loved so much had died. People told her it was God's will. This brought no relief from the gripping hooks ripping at her heart. After all, she reasoned, if this was God's will, He must be a cruel God indeed.

Within a few weeks, she returned to work, still struggling with her loss. A new person, Joyce, started to work at the office and it was Candace's job to train her. However, Candace could barely get through the day, and this added responsibility was too much. She told Joyce about her brother's death and about the terrible time she was having coming to terms with this loss. Hearing this story, Joyce began to cry. Her father had just died, too. Before they knew it, they were both crying. Candace told me, "It was at that second that I felt comfort. I could share my pain. I began to heal. I knew I wasn't alone."

Joyce and Candace became friends. Candace said she felt it was more than coincidence that Joyce had come to her office to work at that time. Candace said, "Maybe God had something to do with it." She learned her spirit was with her brother and that their bond was eternal. Many years have passed, and Candace and Joyce are still friends. Neither one believes that it was only a coincidence that brought them together. They both believe that a higher power guided them.

I have known many people who started out with great doubts about turning their burdens over to a higher power. They really didn't believe that this could work, but once they made the leap of faith to trust to a higher power, they were convinced that this was the way to live their lives.

When people ask me where to begin building this kind of faith, I suggest that they look at a profile of behaviors and beliefs held by people who live their lives this way. Take a look at the following list. You may not believe some or even all of them. But for the next week, act as if they had all been scientifically proven as true. Live as closely as you can by these rules and ideas and see if your life doesn't improve.

People who have turned their burdens over to a higher power have certain beliefs in common. Not all of them believe all of the following, but most believe in the basic principles expressed:

They live as if everything happens for a reason. This reason may not be immediately apparent. But that's okay. By trusting this belief, they don't get burdened down with guilt or disappointment or anger when things don't work out as they had planned. They trust that in time a higher order than they are presently able to understand will make itself known to them. Then the reasons for their early disappointments become clear. Most of us have had experiences that seem to confirm this belief. For example, a relationship ends and you feel broken hearted, but five years later, looking back on it, you realize that if you had stayed in that old relationship, you never would have found the real love of your life a year later.

They accept that the only constant in life is change. Change is a natural part of the order of the universe, and to resist the flow of change is to resist new insights, new learning, and new opportunities in every area of their lives.

They practice being mindful and present in all they do. This simply means that they pay attention to how their own actions affect themselves and the people around them. Do their moment-to-moment actions and thoughts make them happy or unhappy? Do they help them to accomplish what they want to accomplish?

We live by faith or we do not live at all. Either we venture—
or we vegetate. We risk marriage on faith or we stay single.
We prepare for a profession by faith or we give up before we start.

–Harold Walker

28

You Can Depend
on YOU

*Few men during their lifetime come anywhere near
exhausting the resources within them. There are deep wells
of strength that are never used.*

–Richard E. Byrd

Okay, everyone! Get up and stand on your own two feet. In my seminars, I often ask participants to do a simple exercise, which they can do at any time during the day. I ask everyone to stand up with their hands at their sides. I then tell them to stomp their feet, alternating right and left, and at the same time repeat the phrase, "I can stand on my own two feet." I ask them to use a loud, powerful voice while doing this exercise. So come on, reader, get up and do it now! The more often you repeat this exercise, the more self-sufficient you'll become.

When you know you can take care of yourself, you make better choices—ones that are good for YOU. You gain self-confidence. You become attractive to others because you're no longer a needy person, you're a self-reliant one.

Make the desire to be self-sufficient a top priority. How do you do this? There are tools in your happiness kit that will provide some answers. Here are a few nuts and bolts:

- *Spend time with yourself. Get to know your likes and dislikes. Become your own best friend. Treat yourself like a guest.*

- *Remember the times when you survived the loss of a job, a divorce, the loss of a parent or spouse, a major change in your life, or the end of a relationship—and you were okay. You can gain strength from remembering you survived in the past and you will again.*

- *Outfit yourself with a career. Education brings financial freedom. When you can support yourself financially, you gain a sense of pride.*

- *Take time to reflect on your life. It brings awareness of your own strengths. Develop compassion for yourself. Go back to your childhood. Perhaps there were some painful experiences you endured. Look at ALL you've gone through in your life to get to where you are now. Use this to remind yourself that you're a survivor.*

Speaking of survival . . . There are times when we hear of people who have experienced truly terrible trauma. Ruth Nebel, a Holocaust survivor who spent four years in a concentration camp, is one of them. She shared her experience with me.

If you lived through the Holocaust as I did, you're different from other people. You know you can survive anything in life. There was a point when I didn't think I could go on and I wanted to kill myself. Another prisoner came over to me and said, "Ruth, you can always do that." From that moment on, I took each day at a time and I always had hope that maybe tomorrow would be better.

After this terrible experience, it was very difficult to find any happiness again. Today, what makes me really happy are the friends I have selected to be with in my life. A good sense of humor helps. I like to be with people who are happy, not those who get so upset by so many little things in life. I appreciate the little things in life and the things I do for others. Happiness is not something you can pick up on the street. Happiness is in the inside.

Keep Ruth's story in mind when you feel that your life is spinning out of control. Use it as a reminder that when push comes to shove, you can handle whatever comes your way. **You're stronger than you think you are.**

Actress Emma Thompson said she felt torn apart in her private life with the breakup of her marriage, but coping with stress made her stronger than ever. People who've endured suffering

all seem to say the same thing: "I didn't know I was so strong."
They know they can stand on their own two feet because they
have the power to take control of their lives.

To lead a happier life, it's important to KNOW in your gut that
no matter what happens to you, you'll be okay. You can take
care of yourself. And you know what, YOU CAN!!

29

Celebrate Being You!

When what we are is what we want to be, that's happiness.

–Malcolm Forbes

We have everything we need inside us to be happy now. We all have a nugget of gold that gleams and glistens inside us, revealing our magnificence. It may have gotten tarnished from guilt, past pains, and outdated beliefs. The polishing tool for your golden nugget is inside your happiness kit. Take it out and shine yourself up!

I love the poem I received from sixteen-year-old Megan Patton. It's a reflection of the strong and powerful person she feels herself to be.

I AM A TULIP

I am a tulip,
strong and tall with a long, lanky stem.
I am a unique flower
in a bed of roses.
I am my strongest when standing up tall.
I wear beautiful bright petals
that complete me, who I am.

I am the color red.
I am bright and distinctive,
and not like any other color in the rainbow.
I am the color of raging fire,
I am the color of painful blood,
I am the color of sweet roses,
and I am the color of girly lipstick.

I am a diamond.
I am expensive and hard to get.
I need lots of attention and care
to stay my best.
When I am happy I shine and sparkle bright.
I am not like any other gem.

Like Megan, you, too, can become a strong and powerful person.

Celebrate yourself with an internal report card of all A's. You get all A's when you begin to

Accept yourself as you are right now. This is the first step. Ease up on yourself. You're doing the best you can. Many of us think we have to like something or approve of it before we can accept it. That's not true. You don't have to like where you are or your actions to accept them and yourself. You may not like where you are, but accept your position or the direction you've taken, knowing you can change it.

Acknowledge the road you're traveling on. Life may not always be smooth. Rejoice in the fact that you don't give up. Be resourceful and always acknowledge your own creativity in every situation in life. Applaud your strengths and the things you do well. Contemplate what *is* working in your life and do more of it by emulating that behavior.

Appreciate yourself and your environment. Being grateful for who you are and what you achieve in life helps you appreciate yourself. Stop for a moment during each day and appreciate all you do on a daily basis. You're remarkable. Take nothing for granted, especially your good health and the ability to love, laugh, and enjoy your life. You're alive! Look at all the beauty that surrounds you. Listen to the birds chirp, the sounds of the surf or of the wind blowing.

When you recognize yourself as an "A" student, you'll begin to celebrate your own magnificence. You'll treat yourself as the V.I.P.—VERY IMPRESSIVE PERSONALITY—you truly are. You might even throw an "It's good to be me!" party. Invite some guests if you want. Buy yourself balloons. Fly a kite. Do something out of the ordinary, something unexpected, or you can celebrate quietly by taking a solitary hike. You're in charge!!!

The happiest people celebrate even their smallest achievements. These are people who reward themselves when they finish a project. They may take time off or go out and treat themselves to a massage or a bouquet of flowers or a great dinner. These people are happier and more successful than those who don't reward themselves, because they give themselves the message that they deserve success and happiness. Rewarding yourself for reaching milestones connects you to a strong belief in yourself and the fact that you deserve good things.

It's so important to celebrate life in every way and to treasure your trip and the stops you make along the way. Enjoy your scenery. Go ahead, celebrate being you!

30

Be the Captain of Your Own Ship. Stay on Your Happiness Course.

To live we must conquer the seas; we must have the courage to be happy.

–Henri Frédéric Amiel

You're now the captain of your ship. It's easy to drift off course or get lost. Use your happiness compass from your happiness kit and learn to navigate the seven C's of happiness. This is not a chase sequence upon the high seas in some fantasy, action-adventure saga. This is real life, and what counts is your happiness. Stay on course. Here are eight beacons that will light your way and guide you in your happiness direction:

1. *CONSCIOUS. You must be aware of what you're doing at all times. It's too easy to tip over and sink. Study the weather conditions. Be mindful of your actions. Be alert to where you're going and what you're doing. If you find yourself drifting off course, bring yourself back. You're in charge.*

2. *COURAGE—BE GUTSY. Stand by your beliefs. Captains always stay with their ships. Be willing to take risks. Dare to chart your course even if it's different from everybody else's. Sailing into uncharted waters with your happiness compass can bring new excitement and surprises into your life. Maybe you'll find a sunken treasure.*

3. *CHOICE. You always have a choice in every aspect of your life. Choose what's good for you and do more of it.*

4. *CONCENTRATION. Stay focused on what you want to accomplish. Anticipate any rough waters ahead, but don't let them deter you. When you continue sailing in the happiness direction, you'll reach your goal.*

5. *CONFIDENCE. Having self-assurance means that you can handle any obstacle that comes your way. You're a survivor because you have your own mental life jacket on.*

6. *COMMUNICATION—EXPRESS YOURSELF. Tell those on deck what you think. Be straightforward and honest, and at the same time respect their feelings. Don't make anyone guess what you're thinking or feeling. ASK for what you want. If you don't ask for what you want, you'll never get it. Ask and it may become a reality.*

7. *CAPACITY. You have the potential to create fun in your life aboard ship. Everything doesn't have to be so serious.*

Develop a sense of lightheartedness about life. It'll take you to many unknown ports of call.

8. *CULTIVATE. Develop, acquire, and seek lasting relationships with other people on board. Surround yourself with supportive people. After all, we're all in the same boat, sailing the seas together.*

Keep your ship pointed in the happiness direction. Stay on your happiness course. You're the captain of your own ship.

Afterword

Now that you've planted the seeds for your happiness garden, you're ready to reap what you have sown. Your crop has yielded many benefits, and your rewards are healthy, tasty, and bountiful. You've learned ways to feed your soul. You've found balance in your life.

If you wanted a simple answer to finding happiness, perhaps you've now discovered that it's what you DO along the way of your journey that brings happiness. You've weeded out old beliefs, negative thought patterns, guilt, losses, blame, and unrealistic expectations. Perhaps you've replanted with new thoughts and some new friends and fertilized your life with fun and frolic. You've sprinkled enthusiasm and humor on your journey's path. You've stumbled and fallen, but picked yourself up. You've followed nature's wise and beautiful ways. You've reached an oasis of happiness. Take time to sit and see the beauty you continue to create. You've learned to focus on what is RIGHT with you. You can see and feel these results along with the following:

Peace of mind. This is everyone's wish—when your mind is free of clutter and you're relaxed and organized. This keeps you free of worry and ultimately gives you peace of mind.

Empowerment. Happy people know that happiness can only come from within themselves.

Improved health. Studies have shown that happy people handle stress more effectively. Therefore, they have fewer heart attacks and better immune systems.

Abundance. Happy people feel they deserve prosperity, and it comes to them. They're not afraid that there's not enough to go around.

Good sense of humor. Perhaps the greatest asset humans can cultivate is an ability to laugh, even at themselves. This is nurturing because it helps you avoid taking yourself too seriously. There is humor in daily life that needs to be appreciated.

Improved self-confidence. One reason happy people feel confident about themselves is that they're less needy of approval from others. They approve of themselves and rely less on what other people think of them.

Self-esteem. Happy people appreciate and accept who they are. They feel worthwhile and capable.

Focus on the positive. Happy people think about their strengths and what they are good at. They concentrate on what's working in their lives.

Put the necessary time and energy into planting for happiness and you'll undoubtedly have a good harvest. All gardens, however, require maintenance, water, and sun. Give it the care it needs, and then, like a flower, it will bloom with happiness.

About the Author

Willa A. Young is a licensed Marriage & Family Therapist with over twenty years of clinical experience. She is president of the Santa Barbara Council for Self-Esteem and has published numerous articles on self-esteem and happiness. Her popular class, "Happiness Is an Inside Job," has brought Willa much prominence in her field.

As a motivational and inspirational speaker, she faithfully calls attention to the idea that people who look at what's working in their lives, rather than at what's not working, experience more happiness. Her main goal as a facilitator in the field of self-esteem is to get people to feel at least one percent better about themselves. As Willa says, "Even a small gain such as this gives people hope that they can transform themselves into the person they truly want to be."

As an author and motivational speaker, Willa speaks to a number of other themes including:

- *Improving communication with yourself and others*

- *Finding time for yourself in the midst of everyday chaos*

- *Attracting compatible people who are right for you, and improving current relationships*

- *Establishing positive teamwork skills in the workplace*

- *How to unlock inner resources and transform negative thinking into positive action steps*

- *How to heal emotionally from loss of many kinds, such as death, divorce, and job loss*

Willa's guidance for personal change is one of compassion and caring coupled with a wonderful sense of humor.

For more information on Willa Young's presentations, please call 888-480-0880 or 805-899-7333.

Resources for More Happiness

Boorstein, Sylvia. *It's Easier Than You Think: The Buddhist Way to Happiness*. New York: Harper Collins, 1995.

Branden, Nathaniel. *How to Raise Your Self-Esteem*. New York: Bantam Books, 1988.

Carlson, Richard. *You Can Be Happy No Matter What*. San Rafael, CA: New World Library, 1992.

Dalai Lama, H.H. the, and Howard C. Cutler. *The Art of Happiness*. New York. Penguin Putnam, Inc., 1998.

Hay, Louise L. *The Power Is Within You*. Carson, CA: Hay House, Inc., 1991.

———. *You Can Heal Your Life*. Carson, CA: Hay House, Inc., 1987.

Helmstetter, Shad. *What to Say When You Talk to Yourself*. New York: MJF Books, 1986.

Kaufman, Barry Neil. *Happiness Is a Choice*. New York: Ballantine Books, 1994.

Keyes, Ken, Jr. *Prescriptions for Happiness*. Coos Bay, OR: Love Line Books, 1989.

Meyers, David G. *The Pursuit of Happiness*. New York: Avon Books, 1993.

"The Mystery of Happiness: Who Has It...How to Get It." *ABC News Special* with John Stossel. September 4, 1997.

Praeger, Dennis. *Happiness Is a Serious Problem*. New York: Harper Collins, 1998.

Siegel, Bernie S. *How to Live Between Office Visits*. New York: Harper Collins, 1993.

Steinem, Gloria. *Revolution From Within*. Boston: Little, Brown and Company, 1992.

Swindoll, Charles R. *Laugh Again*. Dallas: Word Publishing, 1992.

Quick Order Form

Fax orders: 805-687-2788. Send this form.

Telephone orders: Call 888-480-0880 toll free or 805-899-7333.

E-mail orders: williamsgrp@aol.com

Postal orders: The Williams Group, P.O. Box 3692, Santa Barbara, CA 93130

I would like to order _____ copies of *Happiness Instruction Kit: No Assembly Required* @ $20.00

Name:_____

Address: _____

City: _____State: _____Zip: _____

Telephone:_____

E-mail address: _____

Sales tax: Please add 7.50% for books shipped to California addresses.

Shipping:

US: $4.00 for the first book and $2.00 for each additional book.

International: $9.00 for the first book and $5.00 for each additional book (estimate).

Payment: Check_____ or Money Order_____

Make checks payable to: The Williams Group

For more information on Willa Young's presentations,
please call 888-480-0880 or 805-899-7333.

THANK YOU FOR YOUR ORDER!

Quick Order Form

Fax orders: 805-687-2788. Send this form.

Telephone orders: Call 888-480-0880 toll free or 805-899-7333.

E-mail orders: williamsgrp@aol.com

Postal orders: The Williams Group, P.O. Box 3692, Santa Barbara, CA 93130

I would like to order _____ copies of *Happiness Instruction Kit: No Assembly Required @ $20.00*

Name:_____

Address: _____

City: _____State: _____Zip: _____

Telephone:_____

E-mail address: _____

Sales tax: Please add 7.50% for books shipped to California addresses.

Shipping:

US: $4.00 for the first book and $2.00 for each additional book.

International: $9.00 for the first book and $5.00 for each additional book (estimate).

Payment: Check_____ or Money Order_____

Make checks payable to: The Williams Group

For more information on Willa Young's presentations, please call 888-480-0880 or 805-899-7333.

THANK YOU FOR YOUR ORDER!

Your Happiness Notes

Your Happiness Notes

Your Happiness Notes

Your Happiness Notes

Your Happiness Notes

Your Happiness Notes